food presenting secrets

food presenting secrets

CREATIVE STYLING TECHNIQUES

CARA HOBDAY &
JO DENBURY

PHOTOGRAPHY BY ROB WHITE

APPLE

A QUARTO BOOK

First published by Apple Press in the UK in 2010
7 Greenland Street
London NW1 0ND
www.apple-press.com

Reprinted 2010, 2011 (twice), 2012 (twice)

Conceived, designed and produced by
Quarto Publishing plc
The Old Brewery
6 Blundell Street
London N7 9BH

ISBN: 978-1-84543-335-2
QUAR: GARB

Project Editor Emma Poulter   **Art Director** Caroline Guest

Copy Editor Catherine Osborne   **Designer** John Grain

Proofreader Claire Waite Brown   **Design Assistant** Saffron Stocker

Indexer Dorothy Frame   **Photographer** Rob White

Publisher Paul Carslake   **Creative Director** Moira Clinch

Colour separation by PICA Digital Pte Ltd, Singapore
Printed by Hung Hing, China

10 9 8 7 6

Contents

Parmesan basket, page 110

Chocolate leaves, page 151

Rice presentation, page 114

Introduction

Much has changed over the last 15 years on the world's restaurant scene. On the one hand classic rules are broken, while on the other simple rustic food is championed. The home cook is tempted by the buzz of new ingredients, but a little wary of how to present them.

In this book we have set out to give you the rules of food presentation, or styling, that will allow you to become an artist in your own home. Because that is what a true cook is – an artist who has the skills to allow the freedom of imagination and the ability to translate this to the plate.

Let this book guide you on your presentation journey. On the following pages you'll find all you need to know – from choosing your style of plate and table settings to sourcing the ingredients themselves. Whether you are looking for an interesting way to present everyday vegetables, or a flamboyant sugar display to adorn a dessert, The Technique Directory has a wealth of food styling ideas for you to choose from that will wow any diner.

In the course of a meal, each dish should herald the next, building the excitement before the grand finale of the dessert. With an understanding of the food-presentation formulas that work, you will be able to create beautifully-presented dishes to tempt and excite your guests' palates. Enjoy!

Jo and Cara

About this book

This book is a practical step-by-step guide to presenting all kinds of dishes. With information on the basic rules of presentation, plate choices, table settings and sourcing ingredients, together with a host of presentation ideas, you'll find it easy to add a professional finish to your cuisine.

THE TECHNIQUE DIRECTORY (PAGES 36–153)

Organized into food group categories, this section provides a wealth of food-presentation ideas for you to feast your eyes upon.

The section opens with a visual contents of all the presentation techniques featured.

The level of difficulty is indicated by chef's hat symbols, with one being the easiest and three more challenging.

The clock symbols indicate the preparation time needed for each technique.

Everything you need is clearly identified at the beginning of each technique.

Where appropriate, a list of alternative ingredients to which the technique can be applied is given.

A range of useful tips will help you to succeed.

Each presentation technique is demonstrated with clear and concise step-by-step instructions.

A finished shot presents the result in context.

USEFUL INFORMATION (PAGES 154–171)

In this section you'll find a range of useful information including a resource for selecting edible flowers, shoots and leaves, key recipes referenced in The Technique Directory, a kitchen schedule to help you in the planning of your menu and a weights and measures conversion chart.

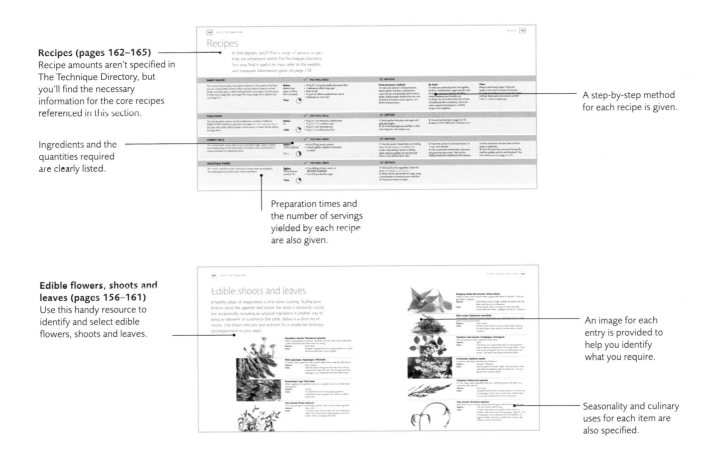

Recipes (pages 162–165)
Recipe amounts aren't specified in The Technique Directory, but you'll find the necessary information for the core recipes referenced in this section.

A step-by-step method for each recipe is given.

Ingredients and the quantities required are clearly listed.

Preparation times and the number of servings yielded by each recipe are also given.

Edible flowers, shoots and leaves (pages 156–161)
Use this handy resource to identify and select edible flowers, shoots and leaves.

An image for each entry is provided to help you identify what you require.

Seasonality and culinary uses for each item are also specified.

BEFORE YOU BEGIN

From pastry sails and herb bouquets to sugar twists and candied flowers, this book is packed full of food-presentation ideas. But before you begin to create your masterpiece, there are a number of things to consider. In the pages that follow, you'll find key information on the basic rules of presentation, plate choices, kitchen equipment, gadgets and table settings. With useful information on sourcing ingredients and helpful pointers on using sauces, foams and oils, you'll find all you need to know to get started right here.

Rules of presentation

We eat with our eyes, gorging on colours and textures, anticipating the flavours to follow. The joy of sitting down for a meal, whether it's with the family or a noisy get-together of friends, is one of life's great rituals: a time to pause, to allow our senses to indulge. But as cooks, it is a chance for us to tempt and tantalize, to show off, if you will, before giving the greatest gift of satisfaction: a plate of food to wow the diner.

But why is presentation important? Because it invites the diner to leave their baggage of daytime hassles behind, to forget their troubles, lift their spirits and to taste, relax and enjoy. If we were to be presented with a plate of soggy blue mush, we would visibly shrink from it. The colour is unpalatable, and we are, after all, hunter-gatherers, primed by our senses to only eat what looks good (and is therefore safe, healthy and not poisonous). Moreover, the texture is unappealing, completely lacking in that satisfying crunch. Food must sing to our senses, call us to the feast and tempt us to devour.

Ultimately there are three key considerations for presentation: set-up, focal point and sauce. Until recently the 'set-up' would be the smiley face – starch at 10 o'clock, meat at 2 o'clock and vegetables at 6 o'clock. For drama, a focal point might be added and elevated and the sauce would be put under, not over, the food. Although these are still good considerations, and we are sure to have come across them before, things have moved forward quite a bit since then.

Here are five simple but nevertheless key points to remember when presenting a plate of food:

BALANCE
Two or three colours are better than one.

SHAPE
Plan for a variety of shapes and forms, not just two. And think about height as a variation.

TEXTURE
Always aim to combine a balance of textures on the plate, but not too many foods of one texture.

FlAVOUR
You can't see flavours, but you need to know how they work together when combining your ingredients.

PORTION SIZE
Make sure you balance the portion sizes with the size of your plate.

Choice of plate

Deciding how to present your food to your guests can be tricky if you're not used to making it look pretty on the plate, but before you begin styling your food, you need to choose what you will present it on. You wouldn't want all your efforts in the kitchen to be ruined by your choice of plate. A plate should complement your food presentation.

A simple rule of thumb is to keep it simple. Your plate choice should work in harmony with the food you're presenting and not compete with or detract from it. Choose crisp white plates (avoid those greyish tones) or very pale colours. Brightly-coloured plates are harder to work with and may clash with some foods or make them look unappetizing. If you want to inject some colour, consider using under-plates to lift the colour scheme of the overall table setting. For example, using a coloured glass or coloured ceramic under-plate will liven up a white tablecloth or wooden table.

When it comes to selecting the shape of your plate, you need to think about things practically. It can be confusing trying to select from the myriad that is available. You probably already have a list of favourite dishes you like to prepare for your guests and undoubtedly have a selection of plates you regularly use for their presentation. If you are ever tempted to try something a little different, here are a few of our favourites that might help inspire you.

1

THE ROUND DINNER PLATE

The bigger the better, but don't go too large for the sake of it, unless you really do have the dining space on the table (your guests shouldn't be cramped). A large dinner plate will frame the food nicely and give you the space to play with. A rim can also be used as a frame for your food.

2

SOUP DISHES OR BOWLS

Choose these carefully. A large rimless dish or bowl can be used to serve a multitude of foods – pastas, noodles and soups – whereas rimmed bowls don't look so good against carbohydrate dishes. Use miniature bowls for holding dipping sauces or small sides on the table.

3

SERVING IN THE PAN

Think about the pan you might use; pale aluminium looks rather good, just make sure you place it on a trivet or a wooden or stone block to prevent burning. If you want to serve individual dishes like this, keep a number of small pans hot and ready to transfer the food to before serving.

4

BANANA LEAVES, CONES AND PAPER CUPS

Banana leaves are simple to present, and look stylish and exotic on the table (see page 115). Paper cups are great throwaway containers to serve food in, particularly desserts, and are very useful if you're having a party since they'll save you time when it comes to cleaning up.

5

THE RECTANGULAR OR OVAL DISH

Rectangular or oval dishes will display simple presentations perfectly, particularly desserts. Dress such plates up with some dainty cutlery, a little sauce or cream pot on the side, or even a small glass of complementary liquor. Such styling techniques are sure to impress your guests.

6

7

8

GLASSES

Glass tumblers or unusually shaped containers are very effective for presenting all manner of foods. They work particularly well for layering different colours and are great for stacking things.

THE SIMPLE WOODEN BOARD

You can never have too many of these in a variety of sizes. Colour is a personal choice and will often be chosen to match your regular table-setting scheme. We favour bleached wood, which works well against green and red foods or grilled meat served on flatbreads. Small chopping boards also make ideal placemats, particularly for a course that might involve two small bowls, containing rice and stir-fry, for instance.

TEACUPS

These are particularly good to use with hors d'oeuvres or desserts, especially if you are serving a small amount of something with an intense flavour. Dress it up with some dainty teaspoons.

9

ICE BOWLS

Ice bowls are a great way to serve chilled food and make your table sparkle with interest. Create bowls decorated with edible flowers (see pages 156–159 for some suggestions), herbs or fruit slices. To make a bowl, you will need two glass or stainless steel bowls; one should fit inside the other with 2.5 cm (1 in) between them. Scatter your chosen flowers or herbs in the large bowl. Place the small bowl inside; tape it to the outside of the large bowl so the rims are flush. Pour water between the bowls to 1 cm (⅖ in) from the top. Add more of your chosen decoration and arrange these using a skewer or similar tool, then freeze overnight. Place the bowls on a kitchen towel and let them stand at room temperature until you can separate them easily. Remove the tape. Lift the top bowl, and invert the bottom bowl to remove the ice bowl. Freeze the ice bowl until you need it. If you are serving food in the bowl that needs to remain dry, set it in a glass bowl within the ice bowl.

10

SERVING PLATTERS

The choice of platters is vast, and there are times when only the grand oval one will do. You may already have your favourites, but here are some alternatives for times when you want to try something different.

Enamelware is a bit of a flashback to the 1950s, but it's a great way of adding a dash of colour to your food presentation, and a smart black rim helps to frame the food. Line it with white parchment paper and use it as a serving platter for roasted meats, or perhaps a tasty chilli crab.

Pewter has a wonderful rustic pallor that offsets strongly coloured food particularly well. Again, it's wise to use parchment paper to give the food a visual lift and prevent any risk of metallic aroma seeping into the food.

Stoneware is another great consideration, particularly marble, slate or pottery. All of these will give your dish extra colour and add texture to the presentation. Stoneware platters are particularly good to use as a backdrop to light-coloured foods.

Equipment and gadgets

Selecting the right tool for the job is crucial, and it comes with experience. When planning to cook up a feast, it's a good idea to make sure you have the right tools – this will make it easier to achieve your desired result.

The greatest of feasts can be created using little more than one gas ring, two pans, a chopping board, a very sharp but small knife and the freshest ingredients. Simplicity is everything when choosing equipment. For example, if we think about chopping – a simple process of cutting miniscule fragments – nothing more is needed than a sharp knife and an absolutely plane and smooth surface, where one can chop without damage. Simple it seems, but blunt machines and dull knives will bruise and damage your ingredients. The point is that to produce satisfying results, choose your equipment wisely and with care, and don't go overboard. It is far better to have three or four good knives that are sharp, well balanced and feel good to handle than a huge array of ill-made equipment that will languish in your drawers untouched. That said, there is without doubt a bare minimum that every good cook must have. These items are shown here.

ESSENTIAL EQUIPMENT

1 Preparation trays: Ensure you have a variety of sizes. Choose trays that are light in weight and will fit in the dishwasher. White plastic is ideal as you can see the colour of the food being prepared.

2 Papers and foils: For a professional finish, make use of parchment paper, cling film, paper towels and aluminium foil.

3 Measuring cup: A cup that's light and easy to clean is ideal.

4 Metal sieve: Metal is better than plastic because it is easier to clean, dry and reuse; however, some plastic sieves will have a finer mesh.

5 Food turner: The old-fashioned, square, flat, metal kind is best because it is thin and flexible.

6 Cheesecloth: This is necessary as a very fine sieve, for jellies and savoury meringues in particular.

7 Bowls: Ensure you have two sizes — choose one very large bowl and one that's quite small.

8 Two teaspoons: For making quenelles (see page 123), choose two of the same size, with a deep bowl.

9 Rings: There are a variety of rings available, although a 10 cm (4 in) pastry ring and 10 cm (4 in) mousse ring are essential — mousse rings are useful for assembling stacked garnishes.

10 Heavyweight metal baking sheets: Sheets that do not buckle at high temperatures are essential. The silicon versions are ideal, but more specialized.

11 Cook's blowtorch: Essential for quick charring, browning or melting food.

12 Rolling pin: For all your pastry needs.

13 Vegetable peeler: For peeling and shaving.

14 Sharp knife and vegetable carving knife set: For all your cutting needs

15 Freezerproof containers: For storage.

16 Whisk: With wooden grip preferably.

17 Parmesan grater: For perfect shavings.

18 Heavy pan: Suitable for making syrup – a copper pan is ideal.

19 Palette knife: For lifting items.

20 Spatula: For spooning, lifting or spreading.

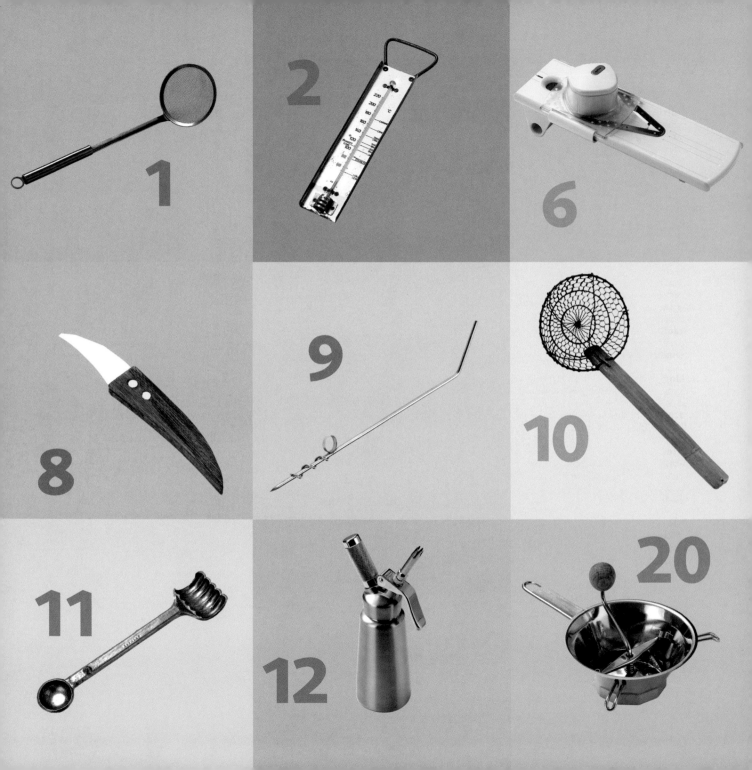

SPECIALIZED EQUIPMENT

The following items are non-essential, but will help you obtain a more professional finish.

1 Tea diffuser: Ideal for deep-frying small items.

2 Sugar thermometer: Convenient, but you can always use the old-fashioned technique of testing by colour.

3 Moulds: A range of moulds is useful. Consider adding the following to your collection:
- Small metal moulds for making filo cups
- Cube mould or similar for resetting chocolate
- Dariole moulds – 55 and 90 ml are ideal.

For jelly, you can improvise with margarine tubs.

4 Pastry cutters: The most useful of all specialized equipment. If you are going to add these to your collection, then 5 cm (2$^{1}/_{2}$ in), 8 cm (3 in) and 15 cm (6 in) cutters are the most practical sizes.

5 Soup ladle: Use this, or similar, for moulding sugar baskets.

6 Mandolin: Specialized device for a range of cutting needs.

7 Julienne peeler: For delicate julienned foods.

8 Turning knife: For turning and shaping fruit and vegetables. A small fruit or kitchen knife can be used as an alternative.

9 Potato spiral cutter: For curly chips!

10 Wire draining spoon: Rather specialized but ideal for deep-frying.

11 Butter curler: For pretty butter garnishes.

12 Metal siphon and CO$_2$ charger: Needed for molecular gastronomy only and therefore non-essential.

13 Milk-frother: For frothy milk and preparing foams and frothed flavourings.

14 Sushi mat: For rolling sushi.

15 Stiff acetate: Use this, or similar, for cutting out tuile or pastry sails. You can use the lid of a margarine tub as well.

16 Scalpel: The only tool that will give you an intricate, clean cut without having to apply pressure. Obtain these from your local art supply shop.

17 Metal ruler: To aid the cutting of perfectly straight edges.

18 Tweezers: Perfect for the handling of small or delicate garnishes.

19 Griddle pan: To add a griddled effect.

20 Mouli-julienne With its assortment of removable discs, the mouli-juilienne is great for slicing and shredding. It's a more primitive form of the food processor.

Although many culinary tasks can be completed with the essential items listed on page 20, there are some specialized pieces of equipment that will aid the finesse of specialized food-styling techniques. Take your time choosing these pieces; spend time in your kitchen deciding what you really need and, crucially, what you feel comfortable with. Opposite you'll find a selection of useful equipment that we have used in this book: use this as reference. Try the gadgets in the shop before you make a purchase: lift them, move them around in your hands – do they feel good? We all have personal preferences when we buy things – whether it be clothing, a car or house – it shouldn't be any different with kitchen utensils. After all, it is only a bad craftsperson who blames his tools, and as cliché as it sounds, ill-made or inappropriate tools should not get in the way of a culinary masterpiece.

Table settings

Setting the scene for what you have prepared is undoubtedly an integral part of any meal. Make your table a feast for the eyes and an inviting setting for your guests to enjoy your food.

The way a table is set establishes the tone of your meal and contributes largely to the ambience of the moment. Whether you want to make it feel like a celebratory meal or a casual brunch, the way you present your food will enhance the atmosphere you wish to create, as well as get your guests in the mood for the courses ahead. Your food should not only indulge the taste buds, but should also be fabulously presented. You'll know you're on your way to a successful meal when your guests' eyes light up with the appearance of each course.

One way to approach a table setting is to evaluate what tableware you already have in your cupboards. Don't go out in a panic and waste time and money on tableware that is not going to be used. It's likely that, like many of us, you've picked up interesting pieces of dishware from kitchen stores and yard sales, and it's perfectly fine to mix and match.

MIX IT UP
The current vogue is very much 'mix and match', so don't feel that you have to restrict yourself to formal matching tableware – why not experiment?

THINK OUTSIDE THE BOX

There's no need to stick rigidly to the rules – put items to different uses. For example, use pint glasses for shrimp and mayonnaise, or dainty little teacups for serving desserts or appetizers (for more, see Choice of plate, pages 14–19). The crucial thing to remember is that you need something to tie all of these mix-and-match elements together. This will prevent your table from looking random and uncoordinated, even if you are aiming for that shabby-chic look.

FIND A THEME

Establish a theme and try to keep it simple. You might want to repeat certain shapes or introduce one main colour that ties all the different elements of your table together. If you were looking to create a Christmas theme for example, red and white are two good colours to start with. Cover your dining table with a crisp white tablecloth, and place a red runner down the centre. Continue the red theme by using red-coloured wine glasses and napkins. Keep everything else simple, with white and clear glass tableware.

For a simple country look, flowers and herbs make the perfect centrepiece decoration. Place neat herbs in matching pots down the centre of your table, so that your guests can enjoy their fresh aroma. Remember, however, that while flowers and other decorations, like candles, will give your dining table a lift, it's important that their height doesn't prevent guests from enjoying each other's company.

SILVER SERVICE
In this simple but stylish table setting, the silver edging of the under-plates is picked out perfectly by shiny silver cutlery. A fruit centrepiece adds a splash of colour to the scheme.

EASY TRICKS

The crucial components of a successful table setting are space, style and simplicity. How you present your food is just as important as the taste itself, and your table settings should complement your dishes rather than overwhelm them. Make sure you have enough space on your table to serve your food, so that it takes centre stage. This is, after all, what your guests have come to enjoy. Here are five easy tricks to help you on your way to table decoration.

1 THINK IN THREES

It's an easy trick, but whether it's three candlesticks or three pretty posies, three always looks better than two when it comes to table centrepieces. And the same rule applies when it comes to mantelpiece and sofa decorations. Try it and see.

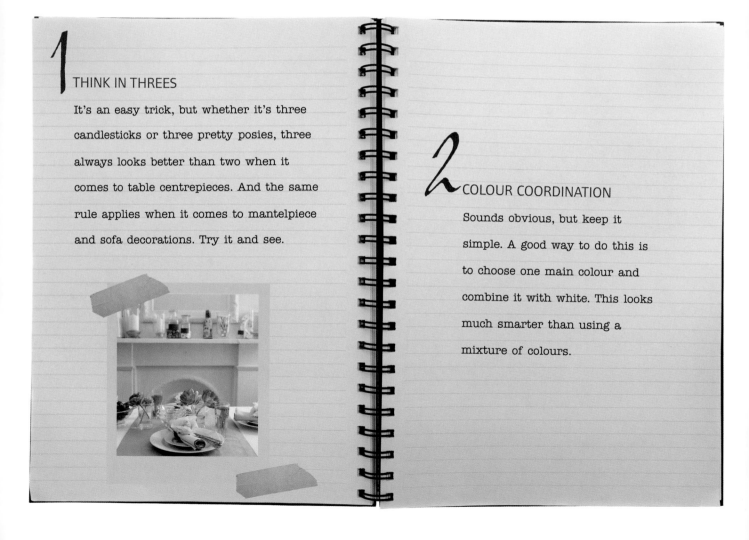

2 COLOUR COORDINATION

Sounds obvious, but keep it simple. A good way to do this is to choose one main colour and combine it with white. This looks much smarter than using a mixture of colours.

3 TABLE LINEN

Keep it crisp and don't skimp on the size of your tablecloth. The rule of thumb is that a tablecloth should hang at 30 cm (12 in) below the table – long enough to hide any ugly bits and not so long that a guest takes the tabletop with them when they tuck their knees under the table. Don't feel you have to stick to a classic white tablecloth – a large vintage linen sheet would do just as well. Similarly, on a lovely wooden table, you may want to use linen placemats for a rustic look.

4 GLASSWARE

Use your glassware and tea sets as serving vessels. We've touched on this before, but delicate sorbets might be best served in a shot glass, and teacups are ideal for anything from soup to desserts.

5 MIRRORS AND LIGHTS

Make use of mirrors to reflect light. This is another little trick that works well with candlelight. Use mirrored tiles as coasters or display your aperitif glasses on a large upturned mirror so that the glass catches the light and shows off your crystal beautifully.

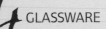

LIGHTING

Lighting can make or break the atmosphere of any room. If it's too harsh, everyone wants to hide, but too dark and no one can see the beauty of the food you have prepared. If you are hosting during the day, especially if you're outside, make sure your dining area is adequately shaded so your guests aren't blinded by the sun's glare.

The key to evening lighting is to keep it low. Candles are a wonderful way of doing this, and can be used indoors or out. Make sure they aren't scented, since strong aromas may conflict with, or detract from, the smell of your food and be off-putting to some guests, especially when eating. Try grouping candles so you have a strong centrepiece of light. If you want to add further interest to your table, use a

SEEKING SHADE
The dappled light of shade shown here is ideal for outdoor daytime dining – it's flattering, your guests won't be blinded by the sun's glare and it will protect your delicious food from the sun's rays.

selection of candlesticks at different heights, but again ensure the height doesn't interfere with the interaction around the table. To create a cosy atmosphere, put fairy lights into vases and place them on your dining table. These will emit a warm, subtle glow, perfect for a romantic dinner for two.

Golden light is the most flattering and can be achieved by using champagne or gold linings in your lampshades. Try to avoid overhead lighting if you can, since it tends to be too harsh and not as calming.

BY CANDLELIGHT
Candles of varying heights line a simple white table setting, emitting soft, subtle light. The blue candlesticks inject a splash of colour into the scheme that is perfect for the evening's atmosphere, and picked out nicely with the addition of blue seat pillows.

Sourcing ingredients

The garnish on your plate is like the cover on a book – it's the first thing that catches your eye and it tells you what to expect. Is it fresh, interesting, innovative? Does it make your taste buds zing with anticipation? The garnish has a huge impact on the success of your dish, so it's worth seeking out the best ingredients to create it.

Back to the roots
The way you present your garnish can suggest freshness – a handful of plump tomatoes on the vine, for instance, will remind the diner that until recently, they were attached to the plant on which they grew.

FRESH IS FABULOUS

The most successful and delicious dishes are those made with really fresh ingredients, and if they are both seasonal and locally-grown then that's even better. Freshness is absolutely essential when it comes to garnishes of fruit, vegetables or herbs. For example, a simple but potentially mouth watering garnish of watercress and rocket – which should make you want to pick it up with your fingers and pop it in your mouth the moment the plate is set in front of you – will lose all its appeal if it's wilted and starting to turn yellow.

GROW YOUR OWN

The ideal way to ensure the freshness of your garnish is to grow your own fruit, vegetables and herbs – it's amazing how much you can raise in a small patch of soil, or in planters. If nothing else you can at least grow pots of herbs on a windowsill, ready to snip when you need them. Growing your own connects you to the restrictions of short growing seasons, which seems to make the produce all the more attractive! And if you love growing flowers, make sure you include a few edible ones (see pages 156–159) – they add colour and an intriguing flavour to salads, desserts and drinks.

FROM THE FARM

An excellent second choice is to track down a nearby 'pick-your-own' farm. This is the closest you'll come to growing your own, and again you'll be inspired to use produce in its natural season. Alternatively, a local farmers' market is a good option, if you're lucky enough to have access to one – it's likely that the produce will have been harvested the day before the market, if not on the day itself. Farm shops are worth looking at, too, but make sure you use one that's well supported and has a high turnover of produce – if it's tucked away out of sight and has no regular clientele, the produce can sit around for quite a while.

THE SUPERMARKET

It might seem like the easy way out, but there's a lot to be said for a good supermarket that sources its produce as locally as possible and has a high turnover.

Store-cupboard garnishes

Pastry
If you haven't time to make your own pastry, you'll find ready-made pastry in the chilled or the freezer section in the supermarket. Pastry garnishes are very versatile and attractive so it's worth keeping a package in your own freezer.

Filo pastry
Filo pastry is usually sold frozen. Crisp filo baskets, cups or even simple squares are great for showing off fillings.

Leaf gelatin
This is usually used for making fruit jellies, so you'll find it in the baking section. As you'll discover, however, vegetable jellies also offer wonderful scope for unusual garnishes in wonderful colours.

Parmesan
If you love pasta or risotto, the chances are you'll usually have a block of Parmesan in your refrigerator as one of the simplest and most effective garnishes. But Parmesan also makes delectable little baskets to fill with vegetables, as well as melt-in-the-mouth wafers that make a really stunning appetizer. You can get away with using a cheaper Parmesan for this.

Rice
Moulds of long-grain rice (not the easy-cook variety) or a mixture of long-grain and wild rice make an impressive garnish, adding height and shape to your presentation. Once you've mastered the art, you can try other varieties such as giant wild rice or Camargue red rice for a really dramatic effect.

Chocolate
Whether you're going to use it for dipping fruit or making chocolate shapes or cups, you need to use good-quality chocolate with a high cocoa-butter content, which will have an appetizing, glossy appearance.

It's also the most likely place to find out of season produce – which, although you should aim to use seasonal produce as much as possible, you will inevitably want on occasion – as well as more unusual items such as banana leaves, samphire and edible flowers.

WALK ON THE WILD SIDE
You can find some of the tastiest leaves and shoots growing wild in the countryside and you'd probably never think of eating them. Dandelion shoots, stinging-nettle shoots and hawthorn leaf shoots, for example, are delicious. Eat them only when they're very young, and remember to wear gloves when picking stinging nettles, because their youth does not make them any less painful. If you can find a source of wild rocket, you'll have a delicious and very attractive garnish available year-round.

Sauces

Sauces are the hallmark of classical French cuisine, a style of cooking that has its roots in the elaborate creations of Marie Antoine Carême (1784–1833), the founder of the haute cuisine concept. Carême not only designed new dishes, he also created new sauces and classified them into groups, based on four mother sauces. These sauces included béchamel, espagnole, velouté and allemande, derivatives of which are used by many chefs today.

These sauces have been cooked using the same ingredients and methods for hundreds of years. Perhaps the only thing that's changed is the presentation of these recipes. Food was traditionally presented on silver platters, and served by waiters using silver-service techniques, with the meat placed at the top of the plate, vegetables to the left and potatoes to the right. In a modern kitchen, the chef presents the food on the plate, which means there's more freedom when it comes to styling. Many chefs will use sauces to create decorative effects, as well as select different plate styles to suit the food they're serving.

Typically, most entrées contain a centrepiece of meat or fish, served with a complementary sauce. The sauce is the cornerstone of haute-cuisine cooking, and can be creamy or stock-based. Some chefs will chose to flood the plate with the sauce, while others will drizzle or drop spots of sauce around the food on the dish. To add extra interest, there may also be a garnish of mousse or turned vegetables.

The unchanging recipes and timeless elegance of this style of cooking and presentation find favour with diners who prefer tradition and luxury, and enjoy the rich textures and subtle flavours of haute cuisine.

On page 32, a red wine reduction is
drizzled for strong lines that echo the
spiral of the carrot strips. On the left,
a flooding of mustard sauce provides
a good base on which to use colour –
in this case, vegetable circles.

USING SAUCES

Thick or thin, every sauce has a role in the dish in which it features, and
its part in the menu is equally important. Carefully flavoured and of
perfect consistency, a sauce should do more than just add moisture: it
should enhance a dish by heightening its flavour, contribute to the colour
of the meal and possibly add texture too. Sauces can also be used to
achieve many decorative effects.

Just as important as selecting the right sauce for your meal is the
serving of the sauce itself – many sauces from good beginnings can
deteriorate when served. To prevent this, it's important to distinguish
between those sauces that can be cooked ahead and kept hot or reheated,
and others that have to be served immediately.

When serving, always heat sauceboats, jugs or dishes before pouring in
hot sauce. Fill the vessel with boiling water and set it aside, then drain and
dry it just before filling.

TIPS FOR SAUCE SUCCESS

1 Never rush the process of sauce making.
Good sauces are the result of time and
care. Whenever possible, use homemade
stock, or be selective about bought
alternatives. Stock cubes vary in quality
some are very powerful and may destroy
delicate flavours.

2 Add any liquid gradually, especially
when there is a danger of lumps forming.

3 Take care when seasoning or adding
flavouring ingredients. A sauce that is
simmered for a long period or reduced
by boiling should not be seasoned to taste
until after it is cooked, since the flavour
will be more concentrated at the end of
the cooking time.

4 If the sauce is to be poured over food,
take care not to drown it. Instead, just
partly coat it and offer the remaining sauce
to diners separately.

5 After serving the sauce, remember to
clean the edges of a serving dish or
individual plate of any drips before taking
it to the table.

Foams and oils

The creativity of the chef has been unleashed into a world unafraid to try new culinary experiences, and supportive of anyone who might want to apply new techniques to old ingredients. Top chefs who are the avant-garde of this movement ensure the dining experience at their restaurants is designed to indulge all the senses, and challenge previously held ideas and norms about food preparation and presentation.

Above, a butterscotch-flavoured cream foam served in a glass dish makes for a contemporary dessert. For details on this technique, see pages 128–129.

Hot and cold foams in particular have become the emblem of this new haute cuisine, and although oils are perhaps less frequently used in haute cuisine, they are unavoidably modern ingredients that deserve recognition. In recent years, the nutritional value of olive oil and other vegetable oils has come to light and consequently these have become an integral part of today's cuisine.

USING FOAMS

The technique by which foams are produced is a product of modern times, where self-taught chefs have broken free of the restraints of formal training, but make good use of the knowledge handed down from their immediate predecessors. This results in a confident reworking of the classics, but would not be possible without modern ingredients and techniques. At the forefront of culinary creativity, this tiny mass of bubbles, that's as light as air, is the product of many experiments, by chefs keen to have haute cuisine recognized as an art form. It's the novelty of these foams that make them interesting to both the chef and diner alike.

A foam encapsulates a sensational taste experience in a small spoonful of flavour, and this simple yet powerful garnishing device can elevate a dish to a whole new level. For those who are confident enough to add foam to their dishes, it is an innovative and creative technique sure to wow your guests. For more on foams, see pages 128–129.

USING OILS

Oils are valued by chefs worldwide for their lightness of texture and subtle flavour. They have been duly incorporated into every creative chef's repertoire of recipes – modern chefs ensure that they have a good array of oils on hand to embellish their latest creations.

Oils that have been infused add a distinctive flavour, but don't overpower other elements of a dish. Extra virgin olive oil, chilli oil, sesame oil, basil oil and garlic oil are just a few examples of these, and can be drizzled over an array of dishes, such as salads, pizzas and pasta. These oils add a subtle undertone of flavour – a hint of spiciness, a touch of zest or an aromatic twist – that can help lift and unite the different textures and tastes of a dish, and really bring the plate alive.

Olive oil is a staple ingredient of Italian cuisine and, depending on where the olives were grown and during which season they were harvested, can either be robust and fruity or light and dry. Olive oil that's used to dress salad has a finer and more delicate flavour compared to olive oil used for cooking, an important consideration when preparing Italian cuisine. Extra virgin olive oil is used to drizzle over salad or as a dip for rustic breads, whereas cheaper olive oils are used for gentle cooking or sometimes even deep-frying.

This freer style followed by many Italian chefs isn't fully embraced by haute-cuisine chefs, who prefer to have control over the addition of oils so as not to spoil the delicate balance of flavours in their dishes. However, most chefs will add a splash of oil before the dish leaves the kitchen, which one could consider as a nod to their Italian counterparts.

1 Olive oil	**6** Black truffle oil
2 Chilli oil	**7** Walnut oil
3 Sesame oil	**8** Tarragon oil
4 Basil oil	**9** Sweet orange oil
5 Garlic oil	**10** Rosemary oil

THE TECHNIQUE DIRECTORY

In this chapter you'll find clear and concise step-by-step instructions to presenting all kinds of dishes. With essential techniques for a range of sweet and savoury accents – from noodle nests and vegetable spaghetti to sugar twists and chocolate flowers, you'll find it easy to add a professional finish to your cuisine.

The techniques

Browse through these visual contents, organized into food groups, to select the food-styling technique you'd like to implement. The chef hats indicate the level of difficulty and the clock symbol the preparation time for each.

PASTRY PRESENTATION

WAFER STACK	PASTRY LATTICE	PASTRY SAILS	PASTRY HOOP	PASTRY BASKETS AND
Page 47	Page 48	Page 49	Page 50	CUPS Page 51

VEGETABLE GARNISHES

SQUARES	CIRCLES	CUBES	CUCUMBER LOTUS	TOMATO ROSE
Page 63	Page 64	Page 65	Page 66	Page 67

PURÉES AND STRIPS

TUILE SHAPES
Page 52

PIPED PURÉE
Page 55

MOULDED JELLIES
Page 56

VEGETABLE STRIPS
Page 58

UNDERSQUARES
Page 60

RADISH ROSE
Page 68

JULIENNE OF VEGETABLES Page 69

SPAGHETTI OF VEGETABLES Page 70

BABY VEGETABLE STILL LIFE Page 72

TURNED VEGETABLES
Page 73

VEGETABLE GARNISHES CONTINUED

VEGETABLE BUNDLES

Page 74

BED OF VEGETABES

Page 76

VEGETABLE BALLS

Page 77

VEGETABLE SORBET

Page 78

FROTHED

FLAVOURINGS Page 80

FRUIT GARNISHES

GAME CHIPS

Page 88

ROLLED GREEN

TOWERS Page 89

VINE TOMATOES

Page 90

FRUIT WAFERS

Page 92

RIND CURLS

Page 93

POTATO TOWER

Page 82

POTATO MATCHSTICKS

Page 83

POTATO SPIRALS

Page 84

FOIE GRAS BONBON

Page 86

FRIED VEGETABLE

STRIPS Page 87

CITRUS PRESENTATION

Page 94

CHOCOLATE-DIPPED

FRUIT Page 96

CARAMEL-DIPPED

FRUIT Page 97

CANDIED FRUITS AND

FLOWERS Page 98

FRUIT FANS

Page 100

BASKETS, BOXES AND CROUTES

FRUITS IN JELLY

Page 101

FILO BASKETS

Page 103

FILO CUPS

Page 104

BREAD CROUTE

Page 106

VEGETABLE CROUTE

Page 107

LEAF GARNISHES

**CLASSIC SPRIGS AND
LEAVES** Page 117

SALAD MOULD

Page 118

BUNCHED HERBS

Page 119

FRIED GARNISHES

Page 120

POTATO BASKETS

PARMESAN BASKETS

TORTILLA BASKETS

NOODLE NESTS

RICE PRESENTATION

DAIRY GARNISHES

BUTTER DISKS

BUTTER QUENELLES

BUTTER CURLS AND BALLS

SOFT-CHEESE QUENELLES

PIPING CREAM

SUGAR GARNISHES

CREAM FOAM

Page 128

ITALIAN MERINGUE

Page 130

FLAVOURED MERINGUE Page 132

SUGAR SYRUP

Page 134

SUGAR WAFERS

Page 135

CHOCOLATE GARNISHES

SUGAR CAGE

Page 142

PREPARING CHOCOLATE Page 145

CHOCOLATE SQUARES

Page 146

CHOCOLATE CUPS

Page 148

SUGAR SHARDS
Page 136

SUGAR STICKS AND TWISTS Page 137

SUGAR SAND
Page 138

SUGAR PLATE DECORATION Page 139

SUGAR BASKETS
Page 140

CHOCOLATE FLAKES
Page 150

CHOCOLATE LEAVES
Page 151

CHOCOLATE FLOWERS
Page 152

CHOCOLATE PIPING
Page 153

Pastry presentation

Whether using ready-made pastry or making your
own, pastry is a wonderful addition to many dishes,
particularly desserts. The simplest of fruit can be
accompanied by a pastry wafer to be enjoyed and relished;
ice cream, when presented with a tuile biscuit can be
elevated to the focus of the plate; and a simple pastry torte can
be given a professional finish with a ring of pastry sails.
The mastery of pastry takes experience and skill, but pastry
decorations are a great way to show off the talent of the cook,
while adding a welcome light and crunchy texture to a dish.

Wafer stack

PRESENTATION

Here, wafers are stacked to add a crunchy texture to layers of creamy chocolate mousse and raspberries. The stack is garnished with raspberry coulis and firm glazed apricots.

→TIPS

- The refrigeration stage is important for best results, because it keeps the pastry in shape.
- These pastry rounds can be made up to three days in advance.

For a fantastic centre plate presentation and a dessert designed to impress, serve whipped cream with fruit or chocolate mousse, or ice cream, between stacked layers of wafer pastry.

1 Roll out the cool pastry evenly and thinly between two sheets of parchment paper. Use light but even pressure on the rolling pin and the pastry once or twice, but do not turn it over. If you feel that the pastry is getting warm and unmanageable, refrigerate it for 10 minutes.

2 When the pastry is approximately 2 to 3 mm (1/8 in) thick all over, peel off the top sheet. Use a well-floured cutter to cut rounds of your required size.

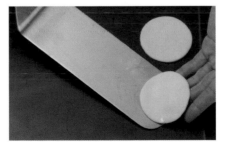

3 Transfer the rounds to a baking sheet, and refrigerate for 15 minutes. There is no need to grease or flour the baking sheet. If you would like a glazed finish on the stack, now is the time to glaze. The stack shown here is unglazed, with confectioners' sugar sifted on.

4 To keep the rounds flat and even in the oven, place another baking sheet on top. You may want to line this with parchment paper. Bake at 200°C (400°F) until golden. When cooked, leave to cool completely before assembling the stack. To serve, layer fruit and ice cream or mousse between each layer.

Pastry lattice

Even though it may look quite intricate, making a pretty pastry lattice to top a fruit pie is relatively simple. Ensure the pastry is cool and take your time, and you'll find your efforts yield a pleasing result.

✔ YOU WILL NEED

- Pastry
- Rolling pin
- All-purpose flour
- Sharp knife
- Metal ruler
- Pastry cutter

PRESENTATION

An individual sweet pastry fruit tart with an attractive lattice top can be served dredged with icing sugar.

→TIP

- To make a buttery pastry perfectly smooth and thin, roll it out between sheets of parchment paper instead of on a floured surface. Use even, light pressure on the rolling pin, and keep turning the pastry to ensure evenness. Do not flip the pastry over.

1 Roll the pastry out to an even thickness. Transfer it to a baking sheet and chill for 10 minutes in the refrigerator. Then lay the pastry out on a well-floured surface and, using a small sharp knife, cut into strips of your required width. We have cut 1-cm ($^2/_5$-in) wide strips.

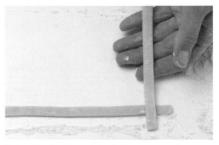

2 Lay the first two strips in the corner of your work surface, the first running horizontally, and the second overlapping the first at a right angle, approximately 2 cm ($^4/_5$ in) away from one end.

3 Now lay the third strip in line parallel to the first, but so the end is over the second strip. To lay the fourth strip, lift up the second strip and tuck the fourth strip under. Repeat the technique with the remaining strips. As the lattice builds, fold back every other strip to lay the new strip down, making sure that it lies in the opposite form to the one next to it.

4 Build your lattice to the size required then neatly cut out a circle using a cutter. If making a larger lattice, use your baking pan to check the size and cut around the edges with a sharp knife. Apply the lattice top and bake until golden. **The pastry lattice tops can be made in advance and stored in the refrigerator.**

Pastry sails

Delicate pastry sails form a nice contrast to whipped cream or rich mousse. Place them on top of the cream, or use them to add the finishing touches to a tart, gateau or torte, such as the raspberry one below.

PRESENTATION

Pastry sails make an attractive presentation for a simple raspberry cream torte, decorated with raspberries and dusted with icing sugar.

➔TIP

- When using a cream filling for the pastry sails tart case, cook the pastry ring up to three days in advance, and make the cream filling on the day. Assemble up to one hour before serving, otherwise the pastry will absorb moisture.

1 Roll out your pastry between sheets of parchment paper, using a light but even pressure on the rolling pin. Roll until thin and perfectly smooth, turning the pastry throughout to ensure evenness. Do not flip the pastry over.

2 To cut the sails out, use a small, sharp, pointed knife and a metal ruler to guide your cutting. Cut out as many triangles as you require – here we used a 10-cm (4-in) wide triangle with 5 cm (2 in) sides.

3 Set the triangles on a baking sheet. Brush with beaten egg or a glaze of your choice. You do not need to grease or flour the sheet. To ensure that the triangles brown evenly and stay flat in the oven, place another baking sheet on top, lined with parchment paper. Bake at 200°C (400°F) until golden.

4 Adorn a dessert by placing individual sails on top of whipped cream, mousse or ice cream or use the sails to border a gateau or tart. After you have cut out the pastry triangles, use them to line the inner edges of a loose-bottomed tart pan. Brush with beaten egg or your preferred glaze. Bake as in step 3. Leave to cool in the pan, then spoon in the mousse. Remove the tart ring then serve.

Pastry hoop

- Pastry
- Rolling pin
- All-purpose flour
- Sharp knife
- 10 cm (4 in) pastry ring
- Metal ruler
- Baking sheet and baking beans
- Parchment paper

PRESENTATION

A chocolate ice-cream ball is presented at the base of the pastry ring and served alongside an orange cream tart.

→TIP

- These pastry hoops can be made up to three days in advance and kept in an airtight container.

Pastry hoops are a simple but interesting way to present the cream or ice cream accompaniment to your main dessert. The quirky way that the pastry hoop is served is easy to create. These rings are also good when made with a tuile paste (see pages 162–163).

1 Roll out the pastry to a thickness of about 3 mm (¹/₈ in), and cut the edges straight. Dust the pastry ring and knife with flour so that the pastry is not dragged. Measure the depth of the ring and mark out its width on the pastry.

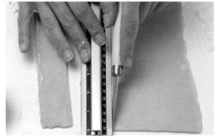

2 Using a metal ruler to guide the knife, cut a length of pastry long enough to line the inside of the ring.

3 Transfer the ring to a baking sheet, and line the inside with the cut pastry length. Using the same technique, line the number of rings required. Refrigerate for at least 20 minutes.

4 Remove from the refrigerator and line each ring with parchment paper. Spoon baking beans into the middle. Bake at 200°C (400°F) for 12 minutes. Remove the beans and parchment and return the rings to the oven for 3 minutes more. Leave to cool completely before serving.

Pastry baskets and cups

For an alternative and attractive way to present a variety of desserts, spoon your fruit salad or chocolate mousse into a pastry basket or cup or use them to hold flavoured or whipped cream accompaniments.

✔ YOU WILL NEED

- Rolled-out pastry
- Metal ruler
- Sharp knife
- 15 cm (6 in) pastry cutter
- Spatula
- Two muffin pans or cup moulds
- Glaze of your choice

PRESENTATION

Once finished, the beautifully golden lattice basket is ready to serve a variety of desserts, or dessert accompaniments.

→TIP

- The lattice will be easier to make if the pastry is very cold. Do not make the individual strips too long, they only need to be 5 cm (2 in) wider than the cutter.

1 Work out how much lattice you will need. One 15 cm (6 in) ring of lattice is needed for each lattice basket. For four baskets, you will need a piece of pastry around 40 cm (16 in) square, cut into 1-cm (^{2}/$_5$-in) wide strips. Cut these strips in half to make 20 cm (8 in) lengths.

2 Each lattice basket is made separately with eight strips of pastry. For instructions on how to make lattice, see page 48. Once you have built the lattice, use a 15 cm (6 in) pastry cutter as a guide and neatly cut four circles.

3 Use a spatula to lift the lattices from the surface into the muffin pan. When positioned over the cups gently push the pastry so it sinks into place. Glaze if desired and bake at 200°C (400°F) for 15 minutes.

Pastry cups

For pastry cups, place your cup mould down onto the rolled-out pastry, and cut around it with a sharp knife. Press the pastry disks neatly into the moulds. Refrigerate for at least 20 minutes, before glazing with egg yolk and baking at 200°C (400°F) until golden.

Tuile shapes

- Stiff acetate, or similar
- Scissors
- Baking sheet
- Parchment paper
- Tuile paste (see page 162)
- Teaspoon
- Rolling pin, or similar, to shape the curved tuile
- Palette knife
- Brioche mould or similar, for the basket
- Springform cake pan for tuile edging

→**TIPS**

- Experiment with different shapes by cutting various stencils, such as stars or initials, diamonds or festive shapes.
- Any size mould can be used to make tuile baskets – try using a tiny cup. You can then fill this with fruit or ice cream as an accompaniment to a main dessert.
- The tuile basket can be the carrier for other things too – mixed summer berries, whipped cream, chocolate mousse, or a fruit and ice cream combination.

Tuile paste is easy to make (see page 162) and extremely versatile. It can be moulded into an array of shapes and sizes. Use these shapes to garnish ice cream or adorn the edge of a delicate tart.

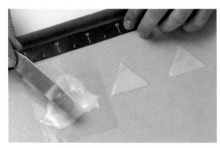

Triangle sails

1 Cut out your stencil (see Shapes of your choice, below). Line a baking sheet with parchment paper and put the stencil on top. Use a palette knife to smear tuile paste over the stencil to an even depth of 0.5 cm (¹/₄ in).

2 Lift off the stencil, leaving a triangular piece of tuile paste behind. Scrape any excess paste from the stencil. Repeat until you have the required number of shapes. Bake at 190°C (375°F) for about 5 minutes until golden.

3 To present tuile sails as part of a dessert dish, shape whipped cream into quenelles (see page 123), and place on the plate. Set three tuile sails in each cream quenelle for an attractive finish.

Shapes of your choice

Stencils for a variety of shapes can be cut out from stiff acetate sheet or plastic lids. In the example above, we have made a triangle stencil for the sails, but squares, diamonds and hexagons are also options.

Round tuiles

For simple round tuiles, take teaspoonfuls of the tuile mix, and drop them onto the parchment-lined baking sheet. Shape into rounds using the back of the spoon. They will smooth out during cooking, but the shape will remain.

Curved tuiles

To make these round tuiles into the classic curved tuile shape you need to mould them around a rolling pin soon after they've come out of the oven. As soon as they are cool enough to handle, but still warm, lift the tuiles from the baking sheet with a palette knife and shape them around the rolling pin using your hand. If they aren't malleable enough, return the tuiles to the oven and reheat them.

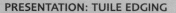

PRESENTATION: TUILE EDGING

To give your desserts a professional finish, first make round tuiles, as shown opposite, but in smaller circles. The size should be approximately 4 cm (1½ in), but no wider than the ring of the loose-bottomed, springform cake pan that you will use for the dessert. Have the ring and an egg white ready when the tuiles come out of the oven. Mould the tuiles around the inside of the cake pan, fixing in place with a dab of egg white, and set aside to cool. Proceed to fill the centre with a fruit or chocolate mousse. When set, remove the ring.

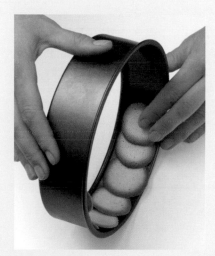

Tuile baskets

Start by making round tuiles – these should be slightly larger than the ramekin you intend to use as a mould. Once baked, lift the warm tuiles onto the upturned ramekin and mould around the sides to form the basket shape. Leave to cool and firm.

Purées and strips

Purées and strips can be used to great effect to garnish
a variety of dishes. They are the main source of colour in a
composition, and provide a wide variety of texture and flavour
too. The projects in this chapter are most effective when used
with root vegetables — their robust nature and starch content
makes them easy to mould into the forms and shapes required.

Piped purée

Piping puréed vegetables is a traditional presentation, that is most effective when used served alongside leafy vegetables, peas or shredded cabbage. Root vegetables tend to be the most effective to pipe.

1 First, boil the carrots in salted water until very tender – this may take up to 15 minutes. Be careful not to overcook them, since this will cause them to lose colour and flavour. Drain the carrots and transfer them to a bowl.

2 Use a hand blender to purée the cooked carrots until smooth. Any larger pieces will block the piping nozzle. Alternatively, use a food mill or a potato ricer on a fine mesh. A food processor doesn't produce a fine enough purée.

→TIP

- Give your piped purée a modern look by varying the size of the nozzle, or piping in spots to give the presentation some form.

3 Fit the piping bag with your chosen nozzle. Hold the piping bag open and fold the top back over your hand while you fill using a spatula. If you have a microwave, the purée can be refrigerated at this stage, then reheated in the microwave when ready to serve.

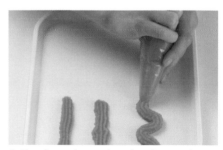

4 Pipe the purée onto hot plates in your chosen design, taking into consideration your plate shape and the other elements of your dish.

Moulded jellies

It is surprising to find savoury flavours used in this
way, but these jellies make for a sophisticated garnish.
Capturing the essence of the vegetable in jellied form
will delight and intrigue your guests.

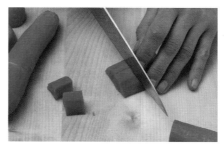

1 Holding the carrot steady with your free
hand, chop into 2 cm (1 in) squares. It is
important to cut the squares small, so that the
cooking time is not too long and flavour isn't
lost. Steam or boil the carrots. Steaming is
preferable, and maintains colour and flavour.

2 Use a conical sieve set over a jug to strain the
purée. Push the carrots through until there is
only pulp left in the sieve. Do not use the pulp
because it will cloud the jelly. Pour one-third of
the purée into a pan and move to the stove.

3 Stir the softened and drained leaf gelatine
into one-third of the purée and heat gently.
Stir constantly until the gelatine has completely
dissolved. Remove the purée from the heat.

4 Stir in the remaining purée. Your purée is now
ready to be jellied. Pour into your chosen dish
and refrigerate until set. For presentation
suggestions, see opposite.

JELLY BALL PRESENTATION

For this presentation you will need to make more jelly than you actually need. To achieve neat, round balls, there is quite a lot of waste created. First pour the jelly into a container that is at least 3 cm (1¼ in) deep, so there's enough depth to scoop out the balls when the jelly is set. Refrigerate to set. When ready, take a melon baller and dip it in hot water. Hold it vertical to the jelly surface and rotate it around a central point to make a nice round ball. It may take a couple of attempts to get this right. Once removed, the balls can be refrigerated until ready to serve.

JELLY MOUND PRESENTATION

Your purée can be poured into any kind of cup, bowl, glass or ramekin to make mounds of different shapes and sizes. Metal moulds are the best for these moulded jellies, but not always available. Plastic moulds work well too, and can be improvised from sauce pots, etc. Pour the purée into the mould and refrigerate to set as normal. To unmould the jellies, have a bowl of hot water ready. Dip the base of the mould into the hot water. Leave submerged for a few seconds, remove and turn over onto the plate. Give the mould a shake and release the jelly onto the plate.

JELLY SQUARES PRESENTATION

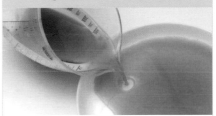

1 If making jelly squares, pour onto a plate to set, making sure the plate is level to ensure an even depth. Put on a tray and refrigerate to set. The tray will make it easier to move the jelly, especially when it is nearly set.

2 Once set, cut the jelly into 2.5 cm (1 in) squares using a ruler or straight edge. Using a palette knife, serve the squares straight from the grid onto the plate.

Vegetable strips

These vegetable strips are a contemporary decoration that will complement almost any savoury dish. They are fun to make and impressive to present. Careful timing and a steady hand is needed for this technique.

YOU WILL NEED

- Carrots
- Hand blender
- Stepped palette knife
- Baking sheet
- Metal ruler
- Scalpel or very sharp knife
- Wooden spoon or dariole mould

ALTERNATIVES

- Beetroot
- Parsnip
- Celeriac

→TIP

- The key to success here is the oven temperature. If it is too hot the strips will brown before drying out. If it is too cool, they will not dry out evenly. An oven temperature gauge is a valuable asset in the kitchen.

1 Prepare the carrots as per step 1 on page 55. Blend with a hand blender for a few minutes on high speed until very smooth. To test, use a palette knife to spread a little on to the baking sheet. It should spread smoothly, without the knife stumbling over any large pieces.

2 Once satisfied with the smoothness of your purée, use the palette knife to lay the carrot purée on the silicon baking sheet in strips, evenly spaced apart.

3 Smooth out the carrot evenly in wide strips using the palette knife. First spread it with the side of the knife across the area of the strip. Next, even out the purée to a uniform depth. To do this, it is important to hold the palette knife level to the baking sheet.

4 Bake at 120°C (250°F) for 15 minutes, or until the carrot is dried out. To remove the strips, use the palette knife to lift them from the baking sheet. They are not as fragile as you may think, so you should be able to do this easily.

5 Transfer the strips to a chopping board. Using a metal ruler as a guide, straighten the edges with a scalpel. Try not to cut away too much of the carrot during this process.

6 To present as a spiral, wind the strips around the handle of a wooden spoon, winding as tightly as you can.

PRESENTATION

The vegetable strips can also be fashioned and baked into a ring to surround a vegetable mousse, a pan-fried vegetable brunoise, a cannon of lamb, or simply to make a neat and attractive container for a vegetable flourish. After drying out the vegetable strips in the oven, press around the base of a lightly-greased metal dariole mould or similar metal mould, and bake for a further 10 minutes. Allow to cool on the mould, or serve immediately.

7 Remove from the wooden spoon handle and set onto your plate, twisting the ends to maintain the spiral form. Set the spirals aside. Cover and refrigerate for up to three days.

Vegetable strips look particularly effective when served with a drizzle of sauce, as shown here. The strips could be used to form a vegetable melange with a vegetable sorbet and a vegetable jelly.

Undersquares

These undersquares make an impressive vegetable presentation that provides a block of background colour and additional flavour to your food, and an interesting texture to your eating experience.

✔ YOU WILL NEED

- Sugar (see vegetable purée recipe on page 162)
- Steamed beetroot (see page 162)
- Hand blender
- Teaspoon
- Small stepped spatula
- Baking sheet
- Large stepped spatula

ALTERNATIVES

- Carrot
- Sweet potato

1 Add the sugar to the steamed beetroot and blend until very smooth using a hand blender.

2 When the consistency is smooth and spreadable, place small dollops of the mixture onto a baking sheet. Make sure they are spaced evenly apart.

→TIPS

- These impressive squares can be made up to five days in advance and stored in an airtight container.
- Beetroot or carrot undersquares will complement most meat dishes – lamb, beef, pork or poultry.
- Carrot undersquares will make a stunning colour for the base of your dish. Use the same ingredients and method as shown for the beetroot undersquares.

3 Use a small stepped spatula or the back of a teaspoon to shape the beetroot mixture into rough squares of an even size and shape, around 10 x 10 cm (4 x 4 in).

4 Use the small spatula to even up the squares and neaten the edges as shown opposite. Hold the spatula perfectly level to smooth out the depth to an even thickness.

PRESENTATION

Creamed and herbed goat's-cheese balls are presented on a beetroot undersquare, which provides a pleasing contrast of colour and texture. The plate is also garnished with radish wafers, purple sancho sprouts and finished with a splash of olive dressing.

5 Bake at 120°C (250°F) for 50 minutes, until crisp. After baking, use a large spatula to lift the squares from the baking sheet and leave to cool.

PERFECTING THE EDGES

For perfectly clean and neat edges, use the edge of the larger palette knife to straighten the sides and make them square.

Use the same method for bigger, rectangular shapes, although larger ones will have to be baked in batches to ensure even cooking.

Vegetable garnishes

Vegetable garnishes will bring flavour, colour and texture to your food presentation. The styling ideas in this section will encourage the diner to look again, as a regular addition on the side of the plate is brought into the limelight by simple but effective presentation techniques. There are, of course, some vegetables that deserve to be centre stage anyway, such as those painstakingly grown miniature vegetables, which are a delight for any table, and impressive with only the minimum of preparation.

Squares

- Sauce of your choice
- Cheesecloth
- Sieve
- Vegetables of your choice
- Vegetable peeler
- Sharp knife
- Olive oil for sautéing
- Paper towels

Adorn your dish by arranging squares of colour in a tile-like pattern or in small groupings as seen here. The presentation can be varied according to the dish you are preparing, and a sauce used for added effect.

1 For the squares, take your selected vegetables and peel off strips of the peel about 1 cm ($^2/_5$ in) wide, and as evenly as you can. For fennel, cut 1-cm ($^2/_5$-in) wide strips of the flesh or stalk. Trim along the side of the strips to even them up. The trimmings can be used elsewhere.

2 Take the even-sized strips and cut into neat 1 cm ($^2/_5$ in) squares. This will have to be done strip by strip, since they can be quite slippery.

3 Take a shallow pan and heat olive oil over a moderate heat. Have paper towels ready to drain the vegetables. Sauté the vegetables for a minute or so, until tender. Drain on paper towels and spoon onto a heated plate. Arrange squares in small groups or in a tile-like pattern.

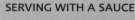
SERVING WITH A SAUCE

If you are adding a sauce to this presentation, you need to ensure it is perfectly smooth. To do this, push the sauce through a sieve lined with cheesecloth. See pages 164–165 for this red bell pepper sauce recipe.

→ TIP

- For best results, it is essential to preserve the colour. When sautéing the vegetables, moderate the cooking temperature to ensure that the colour is not affected, and in the case of olive oil, so that the flavour of the oil is not lost.

Circles

Food styling doesn't have to be complicated to be effective. Inject colour into your dish with a quick presentation of your favourite vegetables that looks extra stylish when the plate is flooded with sauce.

PRESENTATION

A simple game terrine is garnished with circles of colour made from leeks, beans and carrots and flooded with a mustard sauce, for an eye-catching treatment.

→**TIP**

- Fruit can also be used to garnish in this way – try forming circles with orange zests, lime zests, mango strips or papaya. Mango and papaya do not need blanching.

1 Cut green beans in half lengthwise. Cut carrots into thin lengths the same size as the beans. Then prepare the leeks and cut them into thin lengths to match the beans and carrots.

2 Set aside a bowl of iced water. Blanch the prepared vegetables in boiling water, drain well and then plunge into the iced water. This will make the vegetables pliable while helping to retain their colour, flavour and texture.

3 Set the vegetables aside, so they are ready to reheat and garnish the plate. You will find a white prep tray useful for this in order to clearly see the vegetables.

4 Reheat your sauce. Here we have used mustard sauce (see pages 164–165). Reheat the vegetables by plunging them into boiling water for 30 seconds. Spoon the sauce all around the centrepiece of your heated plate and arrange the vegetables in attractive circles radiating out from the centre.

Cubes

This presentation technique involves precision and is a great one for showing off the knife skills of the chef. It is most effective when the cubes are all the same size – the key is to use a very sharp knife.

✔ YOU WILL NEED

- Courgettes
- Yellow pepper
- Onion
- Sharp knife
- Toothpick
- Bowl of iced water

PRESENTATION

Here colourful cubes are used to circle a plate of spinach tagliatelle and tomato sauce and spooned over the top of a shrimp centrepiece to finish.

ALTERNATIVES

Any selection of colourful vegetables will work such as:
- Turnip
- Red pepper
- Tomato
- Carrot

1 First trim the vegetables and cut into even slices, 0.5 cm (1/5 in) in width. This is easier to achieve with root vegetables, such as swedes, but trickier with courgettes. Bell peppers need extra attention to get the slices even and flat.

2 When you have your even slices, stack them one on top of each other and line them up on the sides of your chopping board. Hold them in position using a toothpick. Cut down through the slices to produce even matchstick shapes.

3 Group the matchstick shapes together and, holding them in place with the ends lined up, cut down straight and evenly to get fine cubes of an even size.

4 Blanch the cubes in boiling water for 30 seconds before draining and plunging into iced water. To serve, reheat in boiling water and drain before transferring to your plate.

Cucumber lotus

The Thai art of vegetable carving is quite sophisticated, but if you have the taste for it there are courses that can teach you the art. This simple cucumber garnish makes a pretty plate decoration for canapés.

PRESENTATION

Impress your dinner party guests with a tray of jumbo shrimp, cucumber jelly and mint canapés, garnished with an elegant cucumber lotus.

→TIP

- Vegetable carving sets are available from specialized suppliers. These knives have short blades for maximum control and are sharp and thin, perfect for fine detail.

1 Choose a cucumber with plump, unblemished skin. Halve it lengthwise. If you are making a small number of lotuses, you may want to use only half of the cucumber.

2 Now place the cucumber vertically on your chopping board and make a diagonal cut. The angle should be as sharp as you can make it so that you can create long enough strips for the leaves. Make another diagonal cut parallel to the first one, and about 1.5 cm (³/₅ in) apart.

3 You will now have a piece of cucumber cut at a sharp angle. Working from left to right, make several very straight cuts as close together as you can, but stopping each cut 0.5 cm (¹/₅ in) from the right-hand edge.

4 Now take the first strip and fold it over to form a leaf shape. Continue in this way, curling every alternative leaf around and leaving the others straight, until you have your finished lotus leaf. Cover the lotus leaves with wet paper towels and refrigerate until needed.

Tomato rose

A tomato rose looks complicated, but it's actually relatively easy to make. Use the roses singly as a garnish on a plate of canapés, or for more impact dress your plate with two or three.

PRESENTATION

Party canapés of griddled beef and Parmesan are garnished with rocket leaves and tomato roses.

TIP

- The roses can be stored for up to 24 hours in the refrigerator. Cover a plate with wet paper towels, put the roses on top, then cover with cling film.

1 Select a firm tomato, without bruising. Cut a slice straight across the top, but not all the way. This will create a disk of tomato which will eventually form the base of the rose. Leave a piece 1 cm (²/₅ in) wide still attached to the tomato. This will be the start of the peel.

2 Starting at this point, use a firm and even cut to peel a spiral. Hold the tomato close to the chopping board so that the weight of the cut peel does not break away from the disk of tomato.

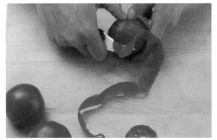

3 Carry on cutting with a steady hand, watching where the knife cuts at the top and bottom. Continue in this way to the top of the tomato until you have a long piece of even peel.

4 Now take the end of the peel and wind it in on itself tightly. Sit the resulting tomato rose on the previously cut disk of tomato.

Radish rose

A radish rose is a traditional garnish for canapés and buffet dishes. Although they are fairly simple to create, the results will vary according to the season and according to what size radish you are using.

PRESENTATION

Here a radish rose provides the finishing touch to a tray of beef fillet and horseradish blinis, finished with flat leaf parsley and a sprinkling of pepper.

→TIP

- For carved vegetable garnishes, you will find a vegetable carving set indispensable. These sets are available from kitchen equipment suppliers.

1 Select a firm, fresh, large radish and cut off the bottom so it will sit flat on the plate.

2 Take your knife and start the first cut about halfway down the radish. Insert the knife without going all the way down. This will make the centre of the first outside petal.

3 Now turn the radish on its side and use the tip of the knife to carve a semicircle with the first insertion as the centre, and the petal being held on at the base. Turn the radish through a quarter turn or a third (if it is small), and make another petal. Work around the radish. The outside petals are the only ones that have a curve.

4 Make the next ring of petals slightly offset to the first ring. You will have to use vertical cuts to form the inner rings without going all the way to the base. Refrigerate in iced water for at least 30 minutes or until ready to use.

Julienne of vegetables

Julienne is simply the French word for vegetables cut into thin strips. The style allows for tasty vegetables; the large number of cut surfaces means a great deal of flavour is released when the vegetables are cooked.

✔ YOU WILL NEED

- Selection of vegetables
- Sharp knife or julienne peeler
- Toothpick
- Bowl of iced water

PRESENTATION

Ready to garnish a main dish, julienne of carrot and swede have been tied in bundles, with chive leaves. For more on vegetable bundles, see pages 74–75.

→TIP

- This cut of vegetables will be most successful if your knives are sharp. Good knives are the most essential part of a chef's toolkit. Professional knives will give the sharpest edge, and therefore the cleanest finish to your vegetable cuts.

1 Slice the vegetable into 0.5 cm (1/5 in) slices. Hold it steady with your free hand and tuck your fingers out of the way. Use a sharp knife to cut down into even slices.

2 Stack a few slices and hold them steady with a toothpick. Slice through the stack to make 0.5 cm (1/5 in) sticks of vegetables.

3 Alternatively, use a julienne peeler to make equal sticks. Hold the peeler steadily and firmly at the top of the prepared vegetable. Apply even pressure and peel downwards, taking care to keep the peeler straight and your fingers out of the way.

4 To cook the julienne, blanch briefly in boiling water, then plunge into a bowl of iced water immediately. Store in iced water until ready to reheat. To serve, reheat the vegetables in boiling water. Drain the julienne and use them to garnish your preferred plate.

Spaghetti of vegetables

✔ YOU WILL NEED

- Selection of vegetables
- Sharp knife
- Julienne peeler or vegetable peeler
- Bowl of iced water
- Oil for frying

ALTERNATIVES

We've used courgettes, carrot and daikon, but other vegetables also work well with this method. Try
- Potato
- Swede
- Parsnip
- Sweet potato

→TIP

- As you peel down, keep the pressure even and the peeler straight. Peel off each layer of spaghetti as you go.

Similar to julienne of vegetables, this is not only an attractive way of presenting vegetables, it is also a tastier way. The many cut sides produce a lot of flavour, and complement a number of entrées.

1 First prepare the vegetables. Trim each one, so that the sides are even and straight. It is important to get the vegetables straight to start with, so that the spaghetti will peel straight.

2 If using a julienne peeler, take a moment to line it up so that it is straight at the top of the cut. If it starts to go wrong at this stage, the lines will not be straight, and the spaghetti will not be attractively long.

3 If there is no julienne peeler available, you can use a normal vegetable peeler to make long, peeled strips. Again, take a moment to ensure the peeler is straight at the top of the cut, so that the peels are long, straight and even.

4 Once you have your spaghetti strips, blanch by immersing them briefly in boiling salted water for 30 seconds. This will preserve the bright colours of the vegetables. Drain well.

5 Have a bowl of iced water ready and put the drained vegetables straight in there.

PRESENTATION

1 For an extra attractive presentation, form the spaghetti into a roll. As soon as the vegetables have been stir-fried and are cool enough to handle, work quickly, taking a handful of strips and draping them over the palm of your hand, lining them up loosely in the same direction. Roll them around so that the ends are on the bottom and the top is made up of striped colours.

2 When you are satisfied with your arrangement, gently position your vegetable spaghetti roll onto the plate. Use your spaghetti roll as a side garnish to the main component of your meal, or as a bed on which to serve it.

6 When ready to serve, heat a little oil over medium heat and stir in the vegetables until they are aromatic and tender, but not browned. Make sure that you don't overheat the vegetables or they will lose their colour.

Delicious slices of pan-fried and glazed lamb are arranged on top of a spaghetti of vegetables, drizzled with a cream and tarragon sauce and garnished with fresh spring thyme sprigs.

Baby vegetable still life

- Selection of baby vegetables
- Sharp knife
- Bowl of iced water

If you are lucky enough to have a supplier of baby vegetables near you, or grow them yourself, this is a very pretty way to present them, resulting in a lovely composition of different shapes and colours.

PRESENTATION

Versatile miniature fennel, miniature red cabbage and the more commonly found baby patty pan squash (in green and yellow) are used to adorn a spring plate.

1 First take your vegetables and soak them in cold water to remove any soil or grit. Leave all leaves on at this point.

2 Trim off any tails or roots. Cut the leaves off close to the base, leaving any tiny curly leaves and a tuft of green leaf on top – this will form part of the presentation.

3 If you are using carrots, they may need some further cleaning. Use a scourer to gently ease off the tougher parts of the skin. Once clean, slice the carrots and baby turnips in half.

4 Halve baby patty pan squash to reveal their white insides and provide a nice contrast with their coloured skins. To serve, blanch your vegetables briefly in boiling water, taking extra care with the leafy tops. Plunge immediately into iced water to preserve the green leafy tops. Drain and arrange around the plate as shown.

→ **TIP**

- Take care to clean the vegetable tops thoroughly to remove any sand or topsoil, without taking away the texture of the vegetables.

Turned vegetables

- Chosen vegetables
- Sharp knife
- Turning knife or paring knife

A classic way of presenting vegetables, this is a chance for you to showcase your knife skills – but try not to be too much of a perfectionist or you'll end up cutting the vegetables away to nothing.

PRESENTATION

The turning technique is a classic way to jazz-up your side serving of vegetables. These vegetables will work wonderfully well with roasted meats.

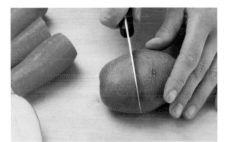

1 Clean your vegetables. There is no need to peel at this stage. We have chosen to use carrots and potatoes. If using potatoes, halve them first.

2 Block off the vegetables by slicing off all curved edges. Trim down carrots or courgettes to form evenly shaped rectangles.

3 Hold a vegetable rectangle in your hand, and take the turning or paring knife in the other hand. Start at the top and make a cut in a moon shape, curving out in the middle and in at either end. Turn one half turn and make another moon-shaped cut. Do not rush the cuts and watch carefully as you cut so you get an even shape.

4 Now continue turning and cutting around the vegetable to make a symmetrical almond shape. It should be narrow and squared off at either end, but should curve outwards in the middle. Repeat with the remaining vegetable pieces. Cook the vegetables using your preferred method, and serve immediately.

→**TIP**

- While turning, you will be tempted to continue cutting to even up the shape and symmetry. Try to resist doing this or you will end up with a very slim vegetable.

Vegetable bundles

For an easy yet elegant vegetable presentation, package your vegetables in neat bundles. Green beans are perfect for this treatment, and teamed with ham they make a graphic statement on the plate.

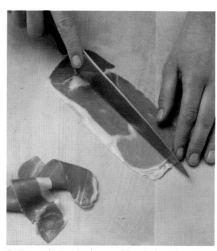

1 To prepare the beans, cut off their stems and cut them into even lengths. To do this, take a bundle of beans at a time, hold them firmly and cut the whole bundle together. Now use this first batch as a guide for the second batch, so that all the beans are of an even length.

2 To tenderize the beans, blanch them briefly in boiling salted water for 30 seconds. Immediately plunge them into iced water to preserve their colour and firmness. Next, cut the prosciutto into slices and into strips of even widths.

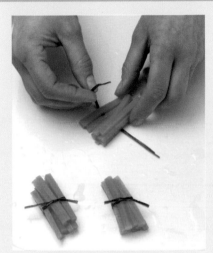

For a pretty presentation of carrots, cut the carrots into matchsticks using the method shown on page 69. Blanch the carrot sticks and chives briefly in boiling water before plunging into iced water. Wrap a piece of chive neatly around each portion-sized bundle of carrots and tie the ends together. Wrap in cling film and reheat prior to serving (see step 4). Chive ties provide a great colour contrast to carrots, but can be used with a variety of vegetables, or as a vegetarian alternative to prosciutto.

3 Wrap a strip of prosciutto tightly around a portion-sized bundle of beans. Then wrap each bundle tightly in cling film. The bundles can be refrigerated at this stage until ready to serve.

4 To serve, reheat each bundle in a sieve over boiling water for 1 minute. Remove from the heat and unwrap the bundles before serving.

A rustic roast chicken is presented on buttered spinach tagliatelle, with charred cherry tomatoes, and green bean bundles.

Bed of vegetables

YOU WILL NEED

- Spinach
- Cheesecloth square
- 10 cm (4 in) mousse ring
- Selection of root vegetables
- Sharp knife

ALTERNATIVES

- Roasted peppers
- Potatoes
- Cucumber for a cold presentation

PRESENTATION

Griddled fillet steak is presented on a bed of spinach with a garnish of diced carrot, courgette and turnip and deep-fried parsley sprigs.

This classic presentation of vegetables is particularly effective when served under a steak so that the vegetables are flavoured by the cooking juices. Cold presentations served over a bed of peeled and sliced cucumber or courgettes work just as well.

For spinach presentation
1 First, boil the spinach in salted water for 5 minutes or until very tender. Drain it well and spoon it into a cheesecloth square. Twist the cheesecloth tightly to extract all the liquid. Set aside.

2 When ready to serve, reheat the spinach in butter over a gentle heat and season well. Set a mousse ring in the centre of a heated plate and spoon the spinach into it. Level it off, remove the ring and set your meat or fish on top. Garnish according to your preference.

For root vegetables
1 Slice the vegetables thinly. Here we have used carrot, swede and potato, and cut into pieces about 3 cm (2 ³/₄ in) across. Season and sauté the vegetables in butter over a gentle heat to preserve the colour.

2 To serve the root vegetables, centre the mousse ring on a heated plate and spoon the sautéed vegetables into the centre of the ring. Remove the ring and set your preferred meat or fish on top of the vegetables.

Vegetable balls

- Selection of vegetables
- Vegetable peeler or sharp knife
- Melon baller
- Sieve
- Bowl of iced water

ALTERNATIVES

- Swede
- Sweet potato
- Pumpkin
- Potato
- Salsify
- Beetroot

Try presenting your balled vegetables in a pastry basket.

For this technique you will need vegetables that are fresh and firm. Older carrots, for instance, tend to go woody in the centre, and the skins of larger courgettes tend to be tough.

1 First choose an appropriate selection of vegetables. Wash, peel and trim them, saving the trimmings for other uses.

2 Take a melon baller in one hand, and the vegetable in the other. Applying firm pressure, insert the melon baller as deep as it will go, and rotate evenly to get a near spherical shape. You may need to practise this once or twice first.

PRESENTATION

Here we have garnished sliced cannon of lamb with carrot, courgettes, swede and potato balls, with a red currant sauce and flat leaf parsley garnish.

3 To cook, boil the vegetable balls briefly in boiling water. Drain the balls as soon as they are tender.

4 Plunge the balls immediately into iced water to arrest the cooking process. This preserves the colour and texture. To serve, reheat in boiling water and use to garnish an appropriate dish.

Vegetable sorbet

An everyday vegetable takes on a new dimension of taste when frozen and presented with other treatments. Turn your favourite vegetable into a sorbet to wake up the taste buds and excite the palate.

1 Follow steps 1 and 2 on page 56 to make a vegetable juice. Pour the cooled juice into a freezerproof tray to a depth of 0.5 cm ($^1/_5$ in). Cover tightly and freeze overnight or until solid.

2 Process the frozen carrot juice until broken down. Add the egg whites and continue to process until smooth.

3 Spoon the processed vegetable purée into a freezerproof container to a depth of 3 cm ($1^1/_5$ in), or the width of the mini scoop or baller.

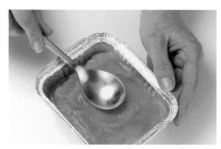

4 Smooth and level the top well and then freeze until solid. Once solid, the sorbet can be presented in a number of ways (see opposite).

BALL PRESENTATION

This is the most popular and versatile way to present the sorbet. To serve as balls, make neat spheres with the mini scoop, cleaning it between each scoop. You may need to practise the technique to get the balls nicely rounded. Once you have carved out your sorbet balls, set them on a plate and freeze for up to 2 hours or until required. Serve on the side of the plate as an accompaniment to a main dish, or as a palate refresher between courses.

SHOT GLASS PRESENTATION

For a contemporary way to present your sorbet, shave into shards using a mandolin or grater and pile into individual shot glasses. Freeze until required.

SORBET SHARDS PRESENTATION

For chunkier, rougher shards, turn the frozen purée block out onto a tray or chopping board, and using a sharp knife, and keeping your fingers out of the way, scrape down to produce iced shards. These wonderfully crunchy shards are great for adding extra texture to your preferred dish. Sprinkle on top of a wafer or in a graphic line along the edge. Also, pile in shot glasses for a contemporary presentation of palate-refreshing sorbet.

Frothed flavourings

These frothed liquids hold a light essence of your flavour. The essence should be strong in flavour, since such a small amount is used, but it needs to be light in texture to be supported in the froth.

YOU WILL NEED

- 100 g (3½ oz) spinach
- Food processor or hand blender
- Cheesecloth
- Measuring jug
- One tablespoon of soy lecithin granules
- Milk-frother

ALTERNATIVES

Spinach is a versatile flavour, but a similar treatment can be given to basil, parsley or other green succulent herbs.

→TIPS

- Soy lecithin is widely available from health food stores
- Beans are often used to flavour frothed liquids, as they are full of starch and produce a good foam that will hold its shape for long enough to be served. A fully flavoured extra virgin olive oil is also a successful flavouring.
- Generally, subtle flavours tend to work better than stronger ones, forming a partnership with the delicate nature of the frothy texture.

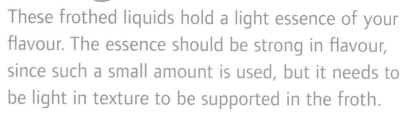

1 Simmer the spinach in boiling water for two minutes. Drain well. Blend in a food processor or using a hand blender. Lay a piece of cheesecloth over a bowl, spoon the spinach into the centre and squeeze out the moisture.

2 Measure out the soy lecithin granules. Pour the squeezed spinach juice into the milk-frother.

PRESENTATION

A frothed spinach and basil swipe is served with slices of sun-dried tomato stuffed chicken, on a bed of red bell pepper purée. For the generic vegetable purée recipe, see pages 162–163.

3 Spoon the soy lecithin granules into the milk-frother. Stir well. Set aside for 30 minutes or so, until the granules have dissolved. Stir well.

4 Ten minutes before serving, heat the liquid gently in a pan, until just under its boiling point. This is when the surface changes slightly, and starts to shimmer. The edges may start to swell, as though the liquid is about to boil. At this stage, put the frother on top and pump up and down vigorously. You will feel the texture changing. Leave to stand for up to 5 minutes. Spoon the froth from the surface onto the plate.

Potato tower

YOU WILL NEED

- Mashed potato
- Sieve
- Butter for greasing
- Mousse ring or similar metal mould, 2–3 cm (1 in) deep, 8–10 cm (3–4 in) wide
- Baking sheet
- Parchment paper
- Spatula

A sophisticated way to present mashed potato, the tower can be garnished using a piquant sauce, or contrasting textured vegetables, such as the chiffonade of cabbage, or with a rich meaty accompaniment.

PRESENTATION

A rolled and stuffed chicken breast is served on a red wine reduction, and accompanied with a tasty golden potato tower, a chiffonade (finely sliced) of cabbage and a sprig of chervil.

1 Mash the potato using your preferred method. Push the potato through a sieve to get the smoothest results for your potato tower.

2 Grease the inside of a mousse ring well with melted butter. Line a baking sheet with parchment paper and set the rings on top.

3 Spoon the mashed potato into the rings and smooth and level the top. Bake for 20 minutes at 200°C (390°F) or until golden.

4 To turn out the towers, remove from the sheet with a spatula and turn over onto the serving plate. Slide off the ring carefully, because it will be hot. Serve immediately.

Potato matchsticks

Liven up the everyday potato and add texture and flavour to a dish with these straw-like fried potatoes. Prepare them in advance or just before serving. Serve loosely or tie in bundles (see page 75).

(see page 75)

YOU WILL NEED

- Potatoes
- Sharp knife
- Mandolin or very sharp vegetable knife
- Preparation tray
- Salt
- Paper towels
- Wire draining spoon
- Oil for deep-frying

PRESENTATION

Ready to garnish a main dish, these tasty potato matchsticks are tied into neat bundles using chives.

1 Peel and cut the potatoes to an even size and use the mandolin to cut into fine matchsticks. If you do not have a mandolin, use a knife.

2 Spread out the matchsticks on a preparation tray and sprinkle over with salt. Set aside for 10 minutes.

3 Rinse the salted matchsticks with water, and spread them out on paper towels to dry.

4 Heat the oil to deep-frying temperature. To test, drop a matchstick into the oil. It should sizzle and rise to the surface. If the temperature is not high enough the matchsticks will be soggy, so be patient. Fry the matchsticks in batches until golden brown. Remove from the oil using a wire draining spoon and keep them warm in the oven.

Potato spirals

Spirals are a fun way to present your potato. They fry up quickly and are sure to delight young and old guests alike. You will need a spiral cutter, which you can buy from a good catering equipment shop.

1 Insert the spiral cutter through the middle of a washed and peeled potato, keeping an equal distance of potato either side.

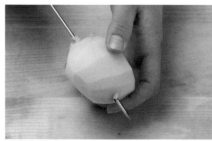

2 Apply fairly firm pressure and start to skewer through the potato.

3 Carry on turning until the hoop of the spiral cutter clears the potato. Maintain a firm pressure and steady hand throughout.

4 To remove the potato spiral, hold the potato firmly in one hand and the skewer in the other and turn the potato around the spiral cutter, using the hoop to hold the potato spiral in place.

5 Gently pull the spiral cutter and the potato spiral free from the potato.

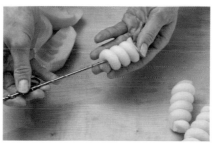

6 Pushing in the hoop, gently remove the cut spiral from the skewer, taking care not to damage the shape of the spiral.

PRESENTATION

Potato spirals add interest to a vegetarian plate of roasted red onion and red pepper, served with a mushroom sauce and pea shoot garnish.

7 Fill a saucepan with corn oil or other suitable deep-frying oil to a depth of 7 cm (2⁴/₅ in) and heat. To check if the oil is at the right temperature, lower a spiral into the saucepan using the wire draining spoon. If it's ready, the spiral will turn golden.

8 Deep fry the remaining potato spirals for 3 minutes or so, until golden brown and cooked through. Drain the spirals on plenty of paper towels. Keep them warm in the oven (100°C/212°F), while you cook the remaining spirals. Season to taste before serving.

Foie gras bonbon

A foie gras bonbon is a great way to add that special finishing touch to a dish. The crispness of the fried potato adds another layer of texture to the dish, while the potato casing preserves the flavour of the filling.

✔ YOU WILL NEED

- Two all-purpose potatoes
- Sharp knife and julienne peeler
- Salt
- Paper towels
- Oil for frying
- Tea diffuser
- Foie gras for the filling

ALTERNATIVE FILLINGS

- Wild mushroom duxelles
- Shellfish

PRESENTATION

Fillet steak is served on a potato rosti base, garnished with flat leaf parsley and presented with a foie gras bonbon.

→TIP

- Ensure that the oil is not too hot, just hot enough, for safe handling, and do not use too much oil. Use a pair of tongs to hold the diffuser if you are concerned about safety.

1 Use the julienne peeler to cut the potato into thin strips, about 2 to 3 mm (¹/₈ in) wide. Alternatively, use a sharp knife to cut the potato into layers. Steady the stack of potato layers with one hand and cut them into equal strips.

2 In a small bowl, mix the potato with a teaspoon of salt and set aside for 15 minutes to soften the potato. Drain and rinse. Squeeze any excess water from the potato and dry off with clean paper towels.

3 Take a tea diffuser in one hand, and put a layer of potato strips in the bottom. Put a small cube of foie gras into the centre and fold the potato over the top. Before you begin frying, have the paper towels ready to drain the potato.

4 Heat the oil to frying temperature. Test the temperature of the oil by dropping in a piece of potato strip. If it sizzles and turns golden instantly, the oil is ready. Holding the tea diffuser with the bonbon inside, fry in the oil until golden and crisp. Beware of the hot oil. Drain on paper towels, and repeat steps 3 and 4 to make more.

Fried vegetable strips

This technique employs the use of a tea diffuser brilliantly. These pretty, tasty orbs of colour are an easy way to enhance a wide range of dishes and give a good graphic shape to arrange on the plate.

Cod fillet is pan-fried until golden and served with black sesame seeds and deep-fried vegetable strips with a swipe of caper crème fraîche.

1 Cut the leeks, potatoes and carrots into long thin strips using a cleaver or a sharp knife.

2 Put all the cut vegetables together in a large bowl and add a teaspoon of salt. Mix well and set aside for 10 minutes. Rinse and drain well. Dry with a clean tea towel or paper towels.

3 Take small amounts of the vegetables, about a tablespoon, ensuring there's a good mix. Put this into the tea diffuser and close.

4 When the deep-frying oil is at the right temperature (see page 83, step 4), dip the tea diffuser into the oil and hold it there for 30 seconds or so, or until the vegetables are golden. Drain on paper towels. Serve hot.

Game chips

These chips are classically used as an accompaniment to game (hence the name) to lighten up velvety sauces. The cross-hatched chips make for an attractive presentation, designed to impress guests.

✓ YOU WILL NEED

- Potatoes
- Sharp knife
- Sharp-edged crinkle cutter
- Oil for deep-frying
- Wire draining spoon
- Paper towels

ALTERNATIVES

- Celeriac

PRESENTATION

Crisp golden game chips are an attractive and tasty accompaniment to many dishes, particularly those with sauces.

1 To create the game chips, you must cut the curved sides of the potato so that they are square and even. If they are not square, the game chips will not be successful.

2 Cut down one side with a crinkle cutter. Discard the first slice. Turn the potato 90 degrees, so that the first crinkle cut is now running horizontally. Make another cut with the cutter. Carry on cutting in this way, turning the potato 90 degrees after every cut.

3 Heat a shallow pan of oil to deep-frying temperature. Test the temperature by dropping a piece of potato into the oil. It should start to turn golden, but not immediately brown. When at the right temperature, use the wire draining spoon to lower the chips into the oil.

4 Deep-fry the game chips, then drain on paper towels. Serve the chips warm.

→TIP

- Some crinkle cutters have a diagonally shaped bottom edge; make sure you purchase a crinkle cutter with a horizontal bottom edge, as this will be easier to manage than other alternatives.

Rolled green towers

 YOU WILL NEED

- Savoy cabbage
- Paper towels
- Cling film

 ALTERNATIVES

- Spring greens or any firm green leaf

PRESENTATION

Here, a stew of spring lamb is served with rolled green towers, while the carrot julienne are presented in neat little bundles.

These rolled towers are an unexpected way to present your leafy vegetables. The secret to a successful tower is to roll up your chosen leaves as tightly as possible.

1 Cook the cabbage leaves in boiling salted water for 5 minutes or until very tender. Alternatively, steam the leaves until tender for about 5 minutes. Drain the cabbage and dry it out on paper towels so it is not waterlogged.

2 To make the rolls, spread out a large piece of cling film on your work surface. Take three cabbage leaves and place them on top of each other so they are slightly offset, spreading them in a straight line away from you.

3 Now roll up the cabbage leaves tightly, pressing in to tighten up the bundle. To make a neat shape, turn in the ends as you go, tucking them into the roll. Wrap one end of the cling film around the bundle tightly, pulling the other end taut, to firm up the roll. Continue to roll.

4 Finish by twisting each end of the cling film. Twist it again tightly, to firm up the shape of the roll and squeeze out any excess water. Chill until ready to serve. To reheat, steam the cling film packages over boiling water. Drain, remove the cling film and serve immediately.

Vine tomatoes

✔ YOU WILL NEED

- Vine tomatoes
- Metal tray
- Olive oil
- Pastry brush
- Cook's blowtorch

ALTERNATIVES

- Bell peppers
- Courgette slices
- Aubergine slices

Charred tomatoes served on the vine and teamed with basil leaves add a splash of colour to this pan-fried sea bass.

→TIPS

- Always store the blowtorch safely, where it will not be knocked over.
- The blowtorch can also be used on some fruits, such as bananas and pineapple, for great decorations to ice-cream desserts.

Charred vine tomatoes make a casual meal special, add a point of interest to the plate and give a simple salad extra flavour. Once you have mastered the safe use of the blowtorch, experiment with a range of vegetables.

1 Set the vine tomatoes on a metal tray or surface. Place some olive oil in a cup.

2 Brush the tomatoes all over with oil, avoiding the stalks and vines.

3 Now turn on the blowtorch, set the gas to high and the flame to medium and ignite it. You need to point the flame at the tomatoes, with the tip of the blue cone, which is the hottest part, making contact with the oiled tomato skin. Ensure that no stalks or vines come into contact with the flame, since the vine will shed black dust.

4 When you turn off the blowtorch, make sure that you turn the gas off and the flame right down. Put on the safety catch for storage.

Fruit garnishes

With its naturally impressive colours and array of
wonderful flavours, fruit lends itself very well to any form
of garnish. A decoration or novel presentation at the dessert
stage of the meal is always particularly welcome. On the pages
that follow, you'll find a range of styling ideas. Making use of a
range of bright shades and interesting textures, these techniques
are both appealing to the eye and the palate.

Fruit wafers

For perfect fruit wafers you need to have impeccable knife skills. To ensure your slices are of an even thickness, use a mandolin cutter. It's also important to get the oven at just the right temperature.

PRESENTATION

Apple and strawberry wafers add the perfect finishing touches to a fruit dessert, decorated with splashes of apricot coulis.

1 Select and clean the apples and strawberries. Slice the apples into wafer-thin slices as shown. Cut the strawberries into slices, but only use the middle slices to create your dried fruit.

2 Brush each slice of apple as you cut with acidulated water to prevent discoloration.

3 Line a baking sheet with parchment paper, and spread out the strawberry and apple slices on it. Bake at 70°C (160°F) for 20 minutes, or until the fruit has dried out without losing any of its colour.

4 Once baked, transfer the fruit wafers to a wire rack and allow to cool. Store for up to one week in an airtight box in the refrigerator. To serve, layer apple wafers in groups on the edge of your dessert plate and arrange strawberries in fans.

Rind curls

A citrus curl placed in the middle of a dessert adds a touch of freshness and sparkle, and is the perfect decoration for a citrus-flavoured dessert. Here, we have used the curls to add party fun to a tray of drinks.

1 Lemons, limes and oranges need to be kept in moist conditions to preserve their texture and flavour. Keep them covered in a bowl of water in the refrigerator. Citrus fruit can also be kept in water at room temperature in a bowl or vase, but make sure you change the water daily.

2 To make your curls, you need a long piece of rind to start with. Use a zester on the side that cuts a single furrow and hold the fruit firmly. Turn the fruit steadily, applying even pressure on the zester. Do not rush, but avoid stopping since this might break the rind.

3 Bring stock syrup to a simmer and immerse the rinds in the syrup. Simmer for at least 10 minutes until the white pith is translucent and the rind is soft.

4 Remove the pan from the heat. When cool enough to handle, wind the rinds around a chopstick or wooden spoon, as shown here. Leave to cool in this position until ready to use.

PRESENTATION

Rind curls make fun and fabulous decorations for drinks, particularly cocktails. Vary the height of the glasses and the colour of the cocktails to add to the fun of the presentation.

Citrus presentation

- Lemons and limes
- Sharp knife or paring knife
- Ice-cube trays
- Griddle pan or barbecue
- Metal tray
- Parchment paper
- Cheesecloth

When it comes to using citrus fruits in the presentation of your food, you'll discover they are very versatile and can be prepared in a number of creative ways, adding a touch of colour and a fresh, zesty flavour to any dish.

Citrus ice cubes
To make citrus ice cubes for drinks, cut small wedges from citrus slices and put them into ice-cube trays. Pour water into the trays and freeze until the ice cubes are ready to use as a refreshing cooler in drinks of your choice.

Lemon wedges
Cut the lemon in half through the middle. On the cut side, make a cut through the centre, towards the edge and through the star pattern. You should have a wedge, with the pith making a star pattern. Each lemon half will give four wedges.

Citrus with a twist
For pretty citrus halves, first remove the seeds with the tip of a knife. Using a sharp knife or a paring knife at an angle, cut a piece of rind all the way around, leaving 1 cm (²/₅ in) uncut, to hold the rind on. Finally, twist the rind into an attractive knot at the edge of the citrus half.

Citrus flowers
Using a knife, trace an imaginary line around the centre of the fruit. Insert the point of the knife and aiming towards the centre, cut a zigzag pattern. Follow the line, keeping the knife aimed at the centre with every cut. When your last cut meets up with the first, pull the two halves apart.

ALTERNATIVE PRESENTATION

Lemons wrapped in cheesecloth

This is a classic presentation, popular with diners because there's no messiness when it comes to squeezing the lemon over the main dish. Simply halve the lemon and place cut-side down in the centre of an 20 cm (8 in) square of cheesecloth. Pull the corners up and twist together at the tip of the lemon. When placing on the plate, rest the lemon on the twist of cheesecloth so it doesn't unravel.

Griddled citrus

For a hearty lime or lemon garnish for broiled or charbroiled dishes, preheat a griddle pan or barbecue and griddle the cut side of a lemon or lime half. For a great effect, use the bars to create a grid pattern on the fruit.

Frozen citrus slices

For a simple but stylish garnish, cut some citrus halves into even slices. Line a metal tray with parchment paper, and lay the slices out. Freeze uncovered for at least 8 hours or overnight. Use within three days.

Here a classic fish treatment, *á la meunière* (tossed in seasoned flour and pan-fried in butter), is classically garnished with lemon in cheesecloth.

PRESENTATION

Arrange the frozen citrus slices attractively to garnish a sorbet. Lemon slices are used here with a blackcurrant sorbet.

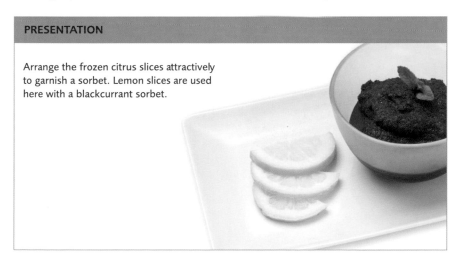

Chocolate-dipped fruit

- Fruit of your choice
- Soft brush
- Dark chocolate
- Non-metallic bowl
- Dipping fork and wire rack
- Paper towels or preparation tray

PRESENTATION

A rich chocolate torte is deliciously accompanied by strawberries dipped in sumptuous dark chocolate.

→TIP

- Dark chocolate is quite unstable and needs careful handling to prevent it 'seizing'. When this happens, the fat and solids separate, and although it can still be used as an ingredient, it is no good for decoration. To prevent this happening, do not allow the chocolate to become too hot. The water should be barely simmering, and use a non-metallic bowl. Do not stir vigorously.

Chocolate-dipped fruit is an all-time favourite, whether garnishing the side of a dessert plate, or presented as a centrepiece. Chocolate fruit is also successful when presented as a dessert canapé for a drinks party.

1 Select fresh firm fruit, such as raspberries, strawberries, mango or peach. Use a soft brush to brush off any dust or debris. Leave the hulls on the strawberries and cut the mango and peach into slices.

2 Meanwhile, melt the chocolate in a non-metallic dish over a pan of barely simmering water. Do not allow the dish to touch the water or become too hot, since the chocolate will seize and become unusable.

3 Take a piece of fruit on a dipping fork and dip into the chocolate, coating half and leaving half bare to show the colour of the fruit.

4 Set a wire rack over a tray or piece of paper towel to catch the chocolate drips and make for an easier clean-up. Set the dipped fruit on the wire rack to drain and cool. Store in an airtight container and use within one day.

Caramel-dipped fruit

Caramel-dipping is enormous fun to do. The technique requires some practice to ensure success – getting the caramel to perfect consistency can prove tricky – but it is extremely satisfying once mastered.

✔ YOU WILL NEED

- Stock syrup (see pages 164–165)
- Pastry brush
- Fruit of your choice
- Dipping fork
- Wire rack

PRESENTATION

Layered puff pastry and cream is topped with strawberries dipped in caramel.

→TIPS

- The temperature of the caramel needs to be regulated to make it easier to work with. If you feel the caramel solidifying and becoming difficult to handle, return it to the heat momentarily, brushing a pastry brush dipped in hot water down the sides of the pan, until it is fluid again. This can only be done three times, before the batch has to be discarded.
- To cut any unwanted caramel strands, move the fruit away from the heat of the pan. As the caramel cools, it hardens and is easier to cut.

1 Heat your stock syrup over medium heat in a heavy-bottomed saucepan. Use a pastry brush dipped in warm water to remove any sugar crystals on the side of the pan, since these will spoil your syrup. Heat the syrup to caramel stage (see page 134), then remove from the heat.

2 Put a clean, dry strawberry on the dipping fork and dip half into the caramel, leaving the hull exposed. As you pull the strawberry out of the pan, sugar strands will form. Holding it at the leafy end, remove the strawberry from the fork.

3 As the caramel runs off the fruit, twist the fork and take up the excess. Return the fork to the pan. For a more adventurous presentation, leave the caramel strands long. To do this, as the caramel runs off the fruit use the fork to pull the strands as they cool, cutting off any excess.

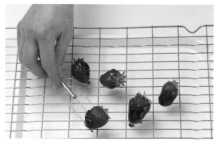

4 Transfer the strawberries to a wire rack to cool and dry. Serve within 2 hours.

Candied fruit and flowers

Candied fruits and flowers are easy to make and use for decoration. A wide variety of flowers are edible — the well known ones are roses, violas and pansies, but so are alpine pinks and daisies.

Candied fruit

- Tinned apricots in syrup
- Sharp knife
- Sugar

Candied flowers

- Salt
- Lemon
- Paper towels
- Two egg whites
- Whisk
- Edible flowers of your choice (see pages 158–159)
- Soft brush
- Two tablespoons of superfine granulated sugar for sprinkling
- Parchment paper

TIPS

- These candied fruits make a great festive decoration on a buffet table, or as part of a dried fruit and nut platter to accompany the cheese course.

Candied fruit

1 Making candied, preserved or glacé fruit is a long process, but a quick version can be made easily from tinned fruit. Take a tin of apricots in syrup and drain off and retain the syrup. Cut the apricots into quarters, and measure the syrup. For every 100 ml (4 fl oz) of syrup add 20 g ($^3/_4$ oz) of sugar, and heat together to dissolve. When the sugar is dissolved, add the apricots to the pan and bring to a simmer.

2 Remove from the heat and spoon into a clean bowl. Set a plate over the surface of the fruit in syrup to keep the fruit submerged under the surface. If there is not enough syrup to cover the fruit, then make some more using 225 g (8 oz) of sugar to about 200 ml (7 fl oz) water. Set aside for 24 hours.

3 Drain the syrup from the apricots again and measure. For every 100 ml (4 fl oz) of syrup add 20 g ($^3/_4$ oz) of sugar, and heat together to dissolve. Add the apricots and heat to a simmer. Repeat step 2. Refrigerate the candied fruit in the syrup for up to five days. Use to decorate cakes and cookies.

CANDIED FLOWERS

1 Ensure that the petals or whole flowers are clean and dry. Some whole flowers, such as roses, will have to be stripped of their base, which is bitter in flavour. Brush off any dust or debris with a soft brush. Once your flowers are ready, degrease a bowl by rubbing salt around the inside with the cut face of a lemon. Rinse and dry with a clean towel.

2 In the degreased bowl, beat the egg whites until bubbles begin to form.

3 Dip the petals into the egg white, or for whole flowers, brush the egg white on with a soft brush. Sprinkle with sugar, and dry on parchment paper overnight. Store in an airtight container and use within two days.

PRESENTATION

Candied rose petals are arranged decoratively to add the finishing touch to a simply iced cake.

Fruit fans

- Avocado, peaches or strawberries
- Sharp knife
- Soft brush
- Acidulated water (see Tip)

PRESENTATION

An avocado fan centrepiece is adorned with a ring of mozzarella balls and delicate cherry tomato fans.

→TIP

- Acidulated water is simply water with lemon juice or vinegar added. Fruits that contain tannin – apples, peaches, avocados and bananas, for example, turn brown when exposed to air. Brush or immerse these fruits in acidulated water as soon as they are cut or peeled.

Fresh fruit needs little preparation and can be used to make very attractive presentations with little effort. Using the freshest and ripest fruits, you can cut them into slices to make these colourful fan shapes.

Avocado fans
1 Peel the avocado carefully, trying not to bruise it. Peel the skin back in pieces using a sharp vegetable knife. Once peeled, brush the avocado with the acidulated water to prevent it from browning.

3 Hold the avocado flat-side down, and position the knife, pointing it towards the stem end and at a diagonal angle to the board. Now draw it back 1 cm (½ in) from the end to make the cut. Make eight more cuts, all radiating from the centre, and stopping 1 cm (½ in) from the end. The avocado slices should be held together at the stem end.

2 To remove the stone from the centre, hold the avocado firmly in one hand, and hold the vegetable knife firmly in the other. Bring the knife down so it embeds into the stone. Gently rotate the knife back and forth to loosen and remove the stone.

PEACHES AND STRAWBERRIES

For peaches, halve and remove the stone and cut the halves into three even pieces. Cut each piece into four slices, stopping short of the end, so that the slices are held together. Handle strawberries in the same way as avocados – point the knife towards the green end and cut across the flesh.

Fruit in jelly

This colourful and flavourful fruit presentation has the added appeal that it can be easily made in advance and stored for up to two days. The jelly can be made in any shape to fit your plate and other garnishes.

PRESENTATION

Summer berries are set in a wine and berry jelly square here and served with raspberry sorbet, fresh berries, mint and sugar sand.

1 Heat the wine and sugar in a saucepan until the alcohol has evaporated and the syrup has reduced slightly.

2 Stir in the berries, and when softened, purée the mixture with a handheld blender. Drain the mixture through a cheesecloth-lined sieve.

3 Take a third of the mixture and heat it through with the softened gelatine leaves. Heat until the gelatine dissolves. Then remove from heat and stir in the remaining mixture. Set the moulds on a tray and fill them halfway with the mixture. Refrigerate for 2 hours or until set.

4 Remove the moulds from the refrigerator. Put a few berries on the bottom layer of jelly. Soften the jelly mixture in a pan set over a gentle heat or in a microwave for 10 seconds at a time. Pour the jelly mix over the berries to the top of mould. Some berries may float. Refrigerate until set.

Baskets, boxes and croutes

If you are looking for a really professional finish, you need to think about what each element of the dish will be wrapped up in, held by or presented on. Presenting a particular element of a meal in a basket, box or croute of some kind, elevates it. If the basket also adds texture to the dish, and appeals to the eye, the eating experience is given added grandeur.

Filo baskets

PRESENTATION

The cucumber and dill sauce to accompany this smoked salmon is served in a filo basket, adding texture and appeal.

Light and very crisp, filo baskets add texture to a dish and make great containers for creams or accompanying sauces. The light quality of the pastry also makes them good packages for baking sweet and savoury fillings.

1 Melt the butter over gentle heat and put to one side with a pastry brush. Take out enough filo pastry for your baskets and return the rest to the refrigerator wrapped in cling film to prevent it from drying out.

2 Lay a sheet of filo pastry on your work surface and brush liberally with the melted butter. Repeat with two more sheets.

3 Cut the pastry sheets into squares slightly bigger than the muffin tray holes. Line the holes with several of the pastry squares, scrunching up the filo attractively around the edges. Bake for 15 minutes at 180°C (355°F).

4 Leave the baskets to cool in the tray and remove with care, so the filo does not chip. Serve with preferred filling.

Filo cups

PRESENTATION

Smoked salmon and crème fraîche served in a filo cup with a dill garnish, cucumber, beet wafer crisps and a sprinkling of paprika. Alternatively, serve this filling on top of some filo wafers (see page 105).

The lightness of filo pastry makes it the perfect choice for party canapés. It is easy to work with, as it comes in sheets, and needs no special treatment, apart from a brush with melted butter just before popping it in the oven. For an extra touch of class, crumple the edges of the pastry to make delicate little cups, a great light snack for hungry guests.

→TIP

- When serving filo wafer canapés, do not use heavy toppings or the wafer will break. Put the topping on your wafers just before serving so they don't go soggy.

1 Make sure you have everything prepared before working with the filo pastry. Melt the butter over gentle heat, and put to one side with the pastry brush. Lay the amount of pastry you require onto your work surface, and return the rest to the refrigerator wrapped in cling film.

2 Lay a sheet of filo pastry onto your work surface and cut into squares large enough to line the moulds with and have some overhanging. Brush liberally with the melted butter. Repeat with another sheet of filo pastry.

3 Next brush the inside of the moulds well with the melted butter.

4 Line the moulds with the filo pastry squares, pushing the pastry down into the bottom and moulding it around the sides.

5 Trim off the excess pastry around the edges with a sharp knife to give the cups an even edge. The filo cups can be refrigerated at this stage if you're not ready to bake them. Otherwise, put the cups in the oven for 15 minutes at 180°C (355°F). Top with a filling of your choice and serve warm. Alternatively, leave them to cool for a cold canapé.

ALTERNATIVE PRESENTATION

To serve canapés on flat wafer sheets of filo, cut the pastry into squares as in step 2, and lay them on a wire rack set over a baking sheet. Bake them as directed in step 5.

Here the same fillings used on page 104 sit on delicate filo wafers.

Bread croute

YOU WILL NEED

- Small loaf of bread
- Sharp bread knife
- Griddle pan
- Pastry brush
- Olive oil for brushing

Sauces to drizzle
- Balsamic reduction
- Mushroom sauce
- Extra virgin olive oil

PRESENTATION

Olive bread is attractively charbroiled and presented with a dish of Parma ham, fig, pomegranate and feta, topped with a balsamic glaze.

→TIPS

- Choose bread with a firm texture.
- A few small slices will look more attractive than larger ones. Choose small loaves with a small slice size.

Bread is a great accompaniment to any dish and with this clever technique, the simplest of foods can be presented with a very professional-looking finish.

1 Take a sharp knife and slice the bread quite thinly and evenly. To get the slices even, you must hold the knife very straight, keeping the blade parallel to the board. You may find it easier with some bread to turn the loaf on its side.

2 Preheat the griddle pan to a medium heat. Brush the slices of bread with oil.

3 Put the bread in the griddle pan so that the charbroiled lines come out at 45 degrees to the straight edge. When the lines are golden brown, turn the bread 90 degrees, so that when finished the charbroiled lines form an evenly hatched pattern on the bread.

4 To store for later use, transfer the bread slices to an airtight container lined with absorbent paper towels. Reheat in the oven at 160°C (320°F) for 10 minutes, and serve with your preferred dish.

Vegetable croute

Vegetable croute is a neat and stylish way to present vegetables. When vegetables are shredded like this, the flavours are more intense, especially once fried.

PRESENTATION

A fillet of red mullet is fried and served over a vegetable croute, watercress and rocket salad, along with asparagus and is drizzled with red pepper sauce.

1 Put the grated vegetables in a draining colander set over a plate to catch the water as it drains. Sprinkle them with salt and stir well. Set aside for 15 minutes.

2 Rinse the vegetables thoroughly in cold water to wash away any bitter juices.

3 Pat the vegetables dry with paper towels. If there is water left on them this will make the fat spit, and reduce the frying temperature. Form loose balls of grated vegetables with your hands, roughly the size of your ring mould. Condense and tighten the balls as much as you can between the palms of your hands.

4 Heat some butter in a skillet over medium heat until it starts to foam. Add the vegetable balls a few at a time and fry for 5 minutes until they are golden and cooked through. Place a ring mould over the balls and slide a spatula underneath the croute. Cut a neat round, allowing the rough edges to fall away in the pan.

Potato baskets

- Two teaspoons of salt
- 2²/₅ lb (1 kg) shredded waxy potatoes
- Paper towels
- Butter for greasing
- Large and small metal moulds
- Spatula
- Two teaspoons of potato flour

There are a variety of ways to serve potatoes with entrées, but you can also create elaborate-looking presentations with them. The potato is a very versatile vegetable and can be paired with many flavours.

1 Stir a teaspoon of salt through the shredded potato to break down the starches and make the potato more pliable. Set aside for 5 minutes, then rinse well under cold running water.

2 Dry the potato well using clean towels. It is important to dry off as much water as possible – any water left on them will make the fat spit and will reduce the frying temperature.

→ TIP

- Potato flour is a valuable standby in any chef's larder. Use it, as here, to hold the grated potato together, or in a potato rosti to give the rosti firmness. It's especially useful to make potato canapés, either rosti or fried.

3 Grease the inside of the large moulds with butter. Grease the outside of the small moulds.

4 Mix the shredded potato with the potato flour. Press the potato mixture into the sides of the large moulds.

5 Push the small moulds into the large ones so that the potato moulds around it. Tidy up the edges of the potato so that it unmoulds cleanly.

6 Bake until golden. When cooked, pick up the mould using a dry cloth or oven glove. Use a spatula to loosen the edges of the potato basket all around the edge. Unmould the basket.

A medley of wild mushrooms is served in a potato basket and garnished with flat leaf parsley, served with frizzled Parma ham, steamed purple sprouting broccoli and a balsamic glaze.

Parmesan baskets

Craft delicious Parmesan cheese into baskets or wafers to add a delicate, crisp touch to your side dishes.

Standard-size baskets
1 Grate the Parmesan on a standard grater. Use a 8 cm (3 in) pastry cutter to sprinkle Parmesan cheese onto a non-stick baking sheet to form Parmesan disks (see step 2 on page 111). Bake the disks for 10 minutes at 180°C (355°F). As soon as the cheese has melted and fused together, remove from the oven.

2 Have a muffin baking tray ready and, as soon as the disks are cooked, gently push them into the muffin holes.

→TIP

- Parmesan is a very high-fat cheese, and as such will burn and stick very easily. Essentially, what you should be doing here is melting the cheese very slightly, just enough for the wafer to hold together, without browning or allowing any of the fat to drain off.

3 Leave to cool completely, before removing them from the muffin tray. Use a spatula or palette knife to gently lift the baskets from the tray. Store for up to three days in an airtight container or serve immediately.

Roasted vegetables are casually served in a crisp Parmesan basket, ready to add colour, flavour and texture to a main dish.

Wafers
1 Finely grate the Parmesan cheese. Use fresh Parmesan for best results. Ready-prepared grated Parmesan will affect the quality of your finished wafers.

2 Take a non-stick baking sheet, and use the cutter as your guide to sprinkle 5 cm (2 in) disks of grated Parmesan. Do not overcrowd the sheet – three or four disks at a time is ample.

PRESENTATION

Stack your chosen filling in between these delicate Parmesan wafers. Here a layered stack of wild mushrooms is garnished with pea shoots and basil.

3 Bake the disks for 10 minutes at 180°C (355°F). As soon as the cheese has melted and fused together, remove the wafers from the oven.

4 Carefully transfer to a wire rack. Leave to cool completely. Store for up to three days in an airtight container.

Tortilla baskets

These baskets are a delicious and impressively attractive way to serve casual Mexican food. Filled with salsa, guacamole or a light salad, they work well as appetizers or as part of a main meal.

PRESENTATION

These delicious golden tortilla baskets can be used to serve a whole host of fillings, but are ideal for serving chilli or presenting tomato salsa as an appetizer.

 TIP

- These baskets can also be made in miniature sizes for parties, or appetizers. Try using larger sizes to serve sauces and relishes in the centre of the table.

1 Take your tortilla wraps and cut them into even 12 cm (4^1/$_2$ in) squares, using a metal ruler and sharp knife.

2 Heat the oil to the correct temperature. Test this with an off-cut from one of the wraps – it should sizzle when it hits the oil.

3 Put one tortilla in the oil. You must shape the basket while it is deep-frying. Keeping your hands clear of the hot oil, use a wire draining spoon to push down in the middle of the tortilla and form the basket shape. Use the base of the pan to form the flat bottom.

4 As soon as the basket is golden, remove it from the oil. Drain immediately on plenty of paper towels and deep-fry the remaining tortillas in the same way. Keep warm until ready to serve.

Noodle nests

Noodle nests are an interesting way to present and liven up a stir-fry. The fried noodle nests work best with egg noodles, but they can also be made with rice noodles.

PRESENTATION

A simple chicken and red pepper stir-fry is presented on a noodle nest, with a garnish of accompanying vegetables.

→ TIPS

- Noodle nests are very easy to do yet yield an impressive result. A wok is ideal for deep frying as the moisture is cooked off quickly, giving crisp results.

1 Cook the egg noodles in boiling salted water or according to package instructions. Remove from the pan with a wire draining spoon.

2 Form a small amount of noodles into a ball, and place a basil leaf on top. Set aside until you are ready to serve.

3 To fry, test the oil with a piece of noodle, when it sizzles it is hot enough. Cook the noodles one nest at a time. Use the wire draining spoon to hold the noodle nest on to the base of the pan, so that a flat bottom is formed. When the nest is golden, use the wire draining spoon to lift it out of the hot oil.

4 Drain off the excess oil on plenty of paper towels. Keep the nests warm until ready to serve. Serve hot, with a stir-fry of your choice.

Rice presentation

Rice is a very versatile food to work with and can be presented in numerous ways to complement your main course. Asian foods are given a lift when accompanied by rice in a steamed banana leaf.

ALTERNATIVE PRESENTATION

Long-grain and wild rice are shaped in a wider mould to form the base for a *salade crevette*, and served with a garnish of pea shoots and a drizzle of salad dressing.

Rice mould

1 For this presentation, the rice can be prepared just before serving, while it's still hot, which is convenient if you do not have many moulds. If you do have enough moulds, it can be prepared ahead of time, stored in the moulds with butter and reheated just before serving. Lightly grease the moulds with butter, and spoon the cooked rice into them. Pack the rice down well to make a tight stack. To reheat, do so thoroughly in the steamer or microwave.

2 Put the rice on the plate before the rest of the dish. To turn out the rice, take the plate in one hand and place it over the top of the mould. Holding both together tightly, turn the plate right side up and give the mould a little shake. Remove the mould to reveal the rice stack.

PRESENTATION

In this particular dish, long-grain and wild rice have been moulded and served with charbroiled shrimp, and a tangy lime salsa.

Rice tower

1 Take a sushi mat and spoon teaspoons of cold rice along one edge. Use your fingers and the spoon to keep the rice in line as best you can.

2 Roll up tightly into a log shape, and store in the refrigerator until ready to use. Make sure you use it within 24 hours.

3 Just before serving, reheat the rice in a steamer or microwave, keeping it in the sushi mat. Remove the rice from the mat and cut the roll into three pieces to serve. Stand them up like towers close to each other.

STEAMED BANANA LEAF PRESENTATION

Cut the clean banana leaf into 10 cm (4 in) wide by 30 cm (12 in) long strips. Put a spoonful of cold rice at one end and fold one corner over, pivoting on the other corner to make a 45-degree angled top. Now fold this triangle down along its bottom edge. Repeat until you reach the end of the banana leaf. Fasten with toothpicks. Reheat in the steamer when ready to serve.

→TIP

- For best results, use natural rice rather than the easy-cook variety. The small particles of dust that are naturally present in this rice will make it easier to mould. For this very reason, do not rinse the rice for too long.

Leaf garnishes

Using leaves is a classic way to garnish and complement a dish. Leaves bring a freshness in flavour to the plate without being the main focus of the dish, and also bring a freshness to the composition. Presenting a dish with some sort of leaf garnish adds life to a plate, and form to a rigid composition – a simple adornment to lift the eye and the palate. The salad presentation shown on page 118 is a stunning but very simple way of presenting greenery, giving height and form to a garnish that is usually quite whimsical.

Classic sprigs and leaves

Garnishing with sprigs and leaves is a simple presentation technique. The success of it relies on the herbs being in top condition. Follow these basic steps for a garnish that will be well received by guests.

✔ YOU WILL NEED

- Selection of herbs
- Preparation trays
- Paper towels
- Cling film
- Salad spinner

PRESENTATION

A salmon fillet is pan-fried and set over creamed potato with a demi-glace sauce. It is served with steamed asparagus and garnished with sprigs of flat leaf parsley.

Single leaves
1 To use single leaves to garnish, pick off your chosen single leaves from the stem.

2 Line a plate with wet paper towels and lay the leaves on it. Cover with cling film and refrigerate until you are ready to garnish.

Classic sprigs
1 Wash the herbs and pick out any stems that have deteriorated. Drain in a salad spinner. To store, line a preparation tray with wet paper towels and lay the herbs on top. Cover with another layer of wet towels, wrap in cling film and refrigerate to keep herbs fresh for two weeks.

2 To use classic sprigs to garnish, pick out sprigs of the desired size and shape and lay out on wet paper towels on a prep tray. Cover with cling film and refrigerate until needed.

Salad mould

- Piece of new 7 cm (2⁴/₅ in) plastic pipe
- Olive oil for greasing
- Pastry brush
- Selection of salad leaves
- Salad spinner
- Salad dressing

PRESENTATION

This elegantly dressed and moulded endive salad will accompany a host of main dishes wonderfully. Finish such a salad with a citrus garnish and a drizzle of salad dressing.

Having something stacked on a plate can look impressive. The organized chaos of the salad leaves shaped into a rounded form will enhance any salad plate and is surprisingly easy to achieve.

1 Wash the pipe before first use. Brush the inside of the pipe with olive oil.

2 Pick over the leaves for the salad and choose those that have a lighter stem or smaller leaves. The salad mould/tower can easily collapse if it becomes unbalanced.

3 Put a small amount of your chosen dressing in the base of a large bowl and toss the salad in so that the leaves are evenly and lightly covered.

4 It is best to put the salad on the plate last, after the other components have been plated. Put the oiled pipe on a plate and pack it with salad. Pack the salad quite firmly so that the shape is solid, but not so firmly that the leaves spring out of the top and bottom. Carefully remove the pipe, leaving the salad in place.

Bunched herbs

- Selection of herbs
- Sharp knife
- Lemon juice or vinegar
- Salad spinner (see Tips, for an alternative method)
- Kitchen towel or paper towels
- Chives

PRESENTATION

Lamb cutlets on a bed of green beans are adorned with classic bunched herbs.

Spring herbs need no extra adornment or preparation to be enjoyed. When prepared properly, the leaves will stay perky and fresh, adding a dash of freshness and colour to any dish.

1 To prepare any herb, first cut off its roots. You can keep these to use later if you wish. Soak the herbs in plenty of cold water. If the herbs aren't particularly fresh, add a splash of lemon juice or vinegar to invigorate them. Drain them well in a salad spinner.

2 To preserve the washed herbs, put them in a large bowl and cover with a clean wet kitchen towel or two layers of wet paper towels. Refrigerate and use as required.

3 To make the pretty bunched herbs for a plate garnish, first prepare the chive ties. To do this, quickly blanch some fresh chives in boiling water until wilted. This will make the chives more pliable. Drain immediately and set aside.

4 Choose some small-leaved sprigs from the stem. Some herbs work better than others — try chervil, flat leaf parsley, fresh spring thyme or fresh chives. Lay the blanched chive tie out flat and arrange your chosen herb leaves in the middle. Bring both ends of the tie up and tie a knot. Trim the chive and stalk ends.

→TIPS

- Herbs preserved like this will keep for up to two weeks.
- If you don't have a salad spinner, wrap the leaves in a clean kitchen towel and shake off any excess water over the sink.

Fried garnishes

- Parsley or coriander
- Paper towels
- Olive oil for deep-frying
- Wire draining spoon

This classic method of presenting herbs adds texture to any leaf garnish. The technique works best with parsley, but you could also use coriander.

1 Select your parsley sprigs, rinse in water and drain well. Pat them dry with paper towels.

2 Heat the clean oil to deep-frying temperature. Drop a little parsley sprig in the oil to check it's at the right temperature. It should sizzle and rise to the surface immediately.

PRESENTATION

Baked river trout is served with julienned potato, and garnished with fried parsley and freshly cut slices of lemon.

3 Deep-fry the parsley sprigs one or two at a time. Do not take them out too soon, otherwise they will become limp after draining. When they are crisp, remove with a wire draining spoon.

4 Drain on plenty of paper towels. Store in a paper-lined airtight container until ready to use.

Dairy garnishes

Dairy garnishes and decorations can be as simple or elaborate as the occasion demands, and can be flavoured with herbs, vanilla or almond extract or laced with fruit purées. Shaping purées and creams into quenelles will give a polished look to a simple dish, and following the guidance given here, you'll be able to pipe velvety cream confidently, for a truly professional finish. To liven up your presentation with unexpected textures and flavours, try using flavoured meringue. It's unexpectedly savoury, with the lightest of textures, and will contrast wonderfully with a rich sauce or reduction of wine.

Butter disks

Butter is a tasty accompaniment often used to enhance vegetables and fish. Below is a simple but classic garnish that can be made up to three days ahead of your dinner party.

YOU WILL NEED

- Butter (8 ³/₄ oz (250 g) serves 8 people)
- Parsley, chopped (4 tablespoons of parsley to 8 tablespoons of butter)
- Grated zest of one lemon
- Salt and black pepper, for seasoning
- Wax paper
- Sharp knife

PRESENTATION

A simple poached fillet of plaice is presented with a disc of parsley butter, which is allowed to melt over the fish as it is served.

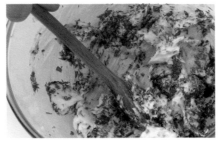

1 Remove the butter from the fridge and leave out until it's slightly soft. Put the butter into a bowl and use a wooden spoon to stir in chopped parsley and grated lemon zest. Season well with salt and black pepper, and ensure all of the parsley and zest are evenly distributed.

2 Spread a 30 cm x 20 cm (12 in x 8 in) sheet of wax paper out flat on your work surface. Spoon the flavoured butter along the middle of the wax paper in a rough log shape. Now roll the paper around the butter, pulling in and tightening up the log shape.

3 Keep rolling and pushing in the ends to make the butter compact. Take either of the paper ends of the log and twist them quite firmly, compacting the log and making it into a well-proportioned shape. Tuck the ends of the paper underneath. Refrigerate until ready to use or for at least 4 hours.

4 To serve, simply unwrap the butter and slice it into disks using a sharp knife.

Butter quenelles

These quenelles add a touch of style to any dish and once you've mastered the shaping technique you'll want to use them again and again. This presentation works best with unsalted butter, which is usually less textured than salted butter.

YOU WILL NEED

- Butter
- Icing sugar
  or maple syrup
- Wooden spoon
- Two teaspoons

PRESENTATION

Serve the quenelles straight from the refrigerator, as an accompaniment to hot desserts. They are especially successful when placed over caramelized apples.

→TIP

- Shaping the quenelles may take some practice, but the trick is to align the spoons before each slide, taking care not to crush the ends of the shape.

1 Remove the butter from the fridge and leave out until it's slightly soft. Beat the softened butter with a wooden spoon until very soft. If using, add the icing sugar and beat the butter until pale.

2 If using syrup, drizzle in a little and stir it into the butter using a wooden spoon. The butter will need to be very soft so it blends well with the maple syrup. Check the flavour and add more as desired.

3 To shape the flavoured butter into quenelles, hold a teaspoon in each hand and align them on top of each other. Hold the teaspoon containing the butter on top and hold the other at an angle. Slide the butter off from back to front.

4 Repeat until the butter forms a smooth three-sided almond shape. Refrigerate the quenelles on a plate until ready to use.

Butter curls and balls

These butter shapes are great for adorning vegetables and fish. Watching these curls form so effortlessly is tremendously satisfying and once a butter curler is in your toolbox, you will find a use for it again and again.

✔ YOU WILL NEED

- Butter
- Flavourings of your choice
- Two food turners or wooden spoons
- Butter curler or melon baller
- Bowl of iced water

PRESENTATION

Balls of parsley butter have been used beautifully to garnish this side dish of Chantenay carrots.

1 Flavour your softened butter (see page 122). Make sure that the flavouring is evenly distributed, then, using two food turners or wooden spoons, shape the butter back into a block – if you use your hands, the warmth will melt the butter! Refrigerate until it is firm.

2 To make butter curls, immerse the butter curler into boiling water. Steady the butter block, and plant the butter curler firmly on the end of the block. Pull the curler back along the surface, making curls as you go.

3 Have a bowl of well-iced water ready. Store the butter curls in here, transferring as you go. Refrigerate until ready to serve.

Butter balls
To make neat balls of butter use a melon baller that has been immersed in boiling water, and shape six even balls from one side of the butter block. Turn over and form six more. Store the balls in well-iced water until ready to serve.

→ TIP

- Leftover flavoured butter can be softened, reshaped and used again. Alternatively, simply use in other dishes as a flavouring.

Soft-cheese quenelles

Soft cheese made flavoursome with the addition of herbs is an excellent appetizer or another tasty component of the cheese course. Shape into quenelles for a simple but impressive way to present soft cheese.

- Selection of herbs
- Cream cheese or soft cheese
- Salt and black pepper for seasoning
- Two teaspoons

PRESENTATION

Goats' cheese is flavoured with chives and chervil and a dusting of pink peppercorns, and served with a swipe of sun-dried tomato and olive caramel, red pepper and caper berries.

1 Chop your selected herbs and mash into the cheese. Season. If the cheese is quite stiff, you'll need to mash it well to make the texture creamy. Otherwise stir well to even out the texture.

2 To make the quenelle shape, hold two teaspoons together in a straight line, with the edge of one spoon at an angle to the edge of the other, and with the bowl of the spoons overlapping. The tip of the bowl of the spoon needs to touch the back of the bowl of the other.

3 Using one of the teaspoons, scoop up one heaped teaspoon of soft cheese. Put the other spoon into position and scoop the cheese forwards, scooping the edge of the spoon along the bottom of the bowl of the other spoon. Keep the spoons in a straight line. Repeat the process a few times to even the shape.

4 Set the completed quenelles on a plate, cover and refrigerate until ready to serve.

Piping cream

Whipped until smooth and light, plump and billowy, piped cream gives everyday desserts a flamboyant finish. Piped onto a tart or gateau, the presentation can be neatly preserved, even on the plate.

1 Take a clean kitchen towel and twist it around into a ring. Place it onto your work surface so it's large enough to hold the bowl.

2 Set the bowl containing the double cream firmly on the folded kitchen towel. If you're using an electric whisk, set it to medium whisking power and check often, since it is easy to over-whip the cream, causing it to separate. Grip the bowl firmly as you whip the cream.

3 Whip the cream until it thickens and soft peaks form. Take care – if you whip it into stiff peaks, it will become separated by the time it is spooned into the piping bag.

4 Prepare the disposable piping bag by snipping off the end to the required thickness, and inserting the nozzle.

To vary the presentation of the piped cream, vary the piping nozzle. A flattened star-shaped nozzle is ideal for piping lines of cream. Below, the cream is piped onto a plate before the dessert is placed in the centre.

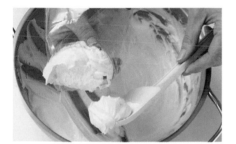

5 Spoon the cream into the piping bag until it is half full. Grasp the piping bag halfway down, and fold the wide end down over your hand.

6 Now twist the top closed, and grip firmly in the gap between thumb and forefinger, as shown. Use the other hand to guide, but not grip, the nozzle.

7 To pipe the cream, hold the bag vertically up from the plate. To form the roses shown, lift the bag as you squeeze from the top. Use the other hand to guide the nozzle.

PRESENTATION

Piping cream attractively adds a special touch to this simple chocolate tart. The tart is finished with a decoration of raspberries.

Cream foam

ALTERNATIVES

In the steps here we have used a fresh mint-infused cream to create a sweetly flavoured foam. A whole host of flavourings can be used, but they must be light enough to be suspended in the foam, with no small particles that will clog the nozzle of the siphon. Alcohol, tropical fruit and citrus flavours should be avoided as they will inhibit the setting ability of the gelatin.

→ TIPS

- There are several methods to achieve the foam, but the one given here is the simplest to achieve without the use of specialized ingredients. The recipe does contain gelatin, however, and so should not be refrigerated for more than 30 minutes for the soft set required. If refrigerated for longer, the cream will be too solid to make a good foam.
- Siphons are available in different sizes. The one used here, which is ideal, is a 500 ml (1 pint) size.
- Since this is a recipe that relies on careful timing, it's a good idea to have a trial run ahead of time, before serving it to your guests.

Chefs everywhere are getting excited about foams. They consist of a single flavour, with a deliciously light, airy texture. With the right tools and technique, they are fairly easy to make.

1 Add mint leaves to cream in a saucepan, and bring to just below the boil – this is called scalding. When you see the surface tension change on the cream, it is ready for step 2.

2 Add the softened gelatin leaves to the flavoured cream, and stir over a medium heat until they dissolve.

3 Place a sieve over a jug and sift the flavoured cream mixture.

4 Pour the mixture into a siphon flask. Shake the siphon vigorously for 5 minutes. This can be tiring so you may want to have an assistant at the ready in case you run out of steam. The key to a successful foam is in the shaking, so it's important that you get this stage right.

5 After 5 minutes of shaking, charge the siphon with the CO_2 charger.

6 Set the flask in iced water to cool or refrigerate for 30 minutes until ready to serve. Spray the foam into your serving dish and garnish further if desired.

PRESENTATION

Dark corn syrup was used to give a butterscotch flavour to the cream foam shown below. The foam is presented in a glass serving dish and decorated with sugar sand and a sugar twist. The foam is served alongside a chocolate drizzle and a mint macaroon.

Italian meringue

Italian meringue is a versatile recipe to have in your repertoire. The egg whites are cooked by the syrup and can be piped in a decorative nozzle or simply spooned over a tart, such as lemon meringue or baked Alaska, as a topping to be served immediately.

✔ YOU WILL NEED

- Pinch of salt
- Lemon
- Large mixing bowl
- 7 oz (200 g) sugar
- Pastry brush
- Sugar thermometer
- 5 egg whites
- Electric whisk
- Raspberries
- Piping bag, either disposable or fabric
- Piping nozzle (not essential if using a disposable piping bag)
- Baking parchment
- Baking sheet

→ TIPS

- This is a two-person operation – you need somebody else to add the syrup in a thin, steady stream, as you keep beating.
- The trick with meringue is to get that wonderful light, airy texture. For the perfect meringue mixture, use a copper bowl for the beating process, which will stabilize and strengthen the egg whites and make the foam firmer.

1 Make sure all of your equipment is grease-free. To do this, clean your utensils as normal and then rub them down with salt and lemon. Sprinkle the salt liberally over the inside of your bowl, and then rub with the cut face of the lemon. Rinse well with water and dry.

2 Put the sugar and water in a suitable pan and set over medium heat to simmer. Brush down the sides of the pan regularly with a clean brush and water. Check the temperature of the sugar syrup with a sugar thermometer and when it reaches 115°C (240°F), start beating the egg whites.

3 Using an electric whisk and gripping the bowl firmly, beat the egg whites until soft peaks form.

4 To test the peaks, lift the whisk from the bowl. Peaks should be clearly visible, as shown.

5 When the syrup has reached 120°C (250°F), or hard ball stage, add it to the egg whites in a thin steady stream, as you keep beating quickly. You may need another pair of hands at this point to pour the syrup into the bowl.

6 When all the syrup has been added, beat at medium speed until the whites have cooled. The meringue will be ready to use when it is thick and glossy, and at room temperature. Flavourings can be added at this stage.

PRESENTATION

Raspberry-flavoured meringue has been piped into thin strips, baked and then used to decorate this blackberry mousse. This is served alongside a raspberry mousse topped with fresh raspberries and garnished with popcorn and pomegranate.

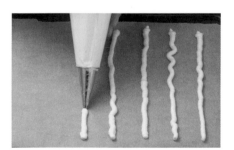

7 To pipe the meringue, spoon it into a large piping bag, and pipe onto a parchment-lined baking sheet. The size shown here will bake at 120°C (250°F) for 20 minutes. The meringues will require more time in the oven if you use a larger nozzle to create them.

Flavoured meringue

You wouldn't expect meringue to be served with a savory dish, but mix it with complementary flavours to make a surprisingly tasty accompaniment, along with providing texture to a dish.

PRESENTATION

Here, we have garnished smoked trout fillet with an open beetroot and horseradish tart, and a beetroot meringue.

1 Pour the measured tepid beetroot juice (see steps 1–3 of the savoury meringue on page 165) onto the dried egg white in the base of a large clean mixing bowl.

2 Use a whisk to beat together the egg white and juice until frothy and well blended. Cover tightly with cling film, and refrigerate for 4 hours or overnight.

3 When ready to bake the meringues, remove them from the refrigerator and beat the rehydrated egg whites until they form stiff peaks. Preheat the oven to 90°C (195°F).

4 Use two dessertspoons to shape the meringue into quenelles, or egg shapes (see steps 2–3, page 125). Place immediately onto the parchment paper or silicon mat, and bake for 1 hour 30 minutes. Use one or two to garnish a side plate. Meringues can be stored in an airtight container for up to three days.

Sugar garnishes

All courses can be garnished and presented to please
the eye and palate, but none reach the fanciful heights of
the sugar decoration. Sugar decorations are pure confections
of pleasure, designed to excite the senses. The magic of spun
sugar creations is a wonder of kitchen chemistry and the thrill of
mastering it can be just as thrilling as being presented with a dish
that is garnished with a sugar creation. Work your way through the
chapter, gaining confidence with each project, and you will soon be
designing and making your own sugar masterpieces.

Sugar syrup

- Sugar (see stock syrup, page 164)
- Heavy pan (a copper pan is ideal)
- Pastry brush
- Large bowl of iced water
- Sugar thermometer

PRESENTATION

Raspberry mousse is decorated with Italian meringue and fresh raspberries and presented on a plate drizzled with caramel syrup. As a finishing touch, the plate has been garnished with popped corn and chopped pistachios.

→**TIP**

- You must not forget that the syrup is extremely hot, and to prevent injury or burns, you must handle both the pan and the syrup with care, using an oven glove at all times.

Syrup cooked to 165°C (330°F) and to the caramel stage can be worked in a number of ways before it cools and hardens. It requires skill and dexterity for the more complex projects, but there are simpler ones that can be achieved with only a little practice.

1 Put the sugar and water together in a heavy pan and set over medium heat to boil. Do not put too much heat under the pan; if the sides of the pan get too hot, the sugar will crystallize and the batch will have to be discarded.

2 To avoid any crystals forming, use a pastry brush to wash down the sides of the pan with water every few minutes. Have a large bowl of iced water ready.

3 Warm a sugar thermometer in a jug of hot water and place the thermometer in the pan of syrup to monitor the temperature. For caramel, boil the syrup rapidly until the temperature reaches 165°C (330°F). If you are using the syrup for other purposes, stop the cooking at the desired temperature.

4 When 165°C (330°F) has been reached, the syrup will be a caramel colour as shown here. Immediately plunge the base of the pan into the iced water to prevent the syrup from cooking further and burning.

Sugar wafers

✔ YOU WILL NEED

- Sugar syrup base (see page 134)
- Heavy pan (a copper pan is ideal)
- Pastry brush
- Sugar thermometer
- Baking sheet
- Parchment paper
- Large bowl of iced water

Sugar wafers are very delicate and so require a steady, gentle hand. They can be used to decorate many desserts and are great for taking the edge off sharp fruits. As with many sugar decorations, they can only be kept for one day in an airtight container.

PRESENTATION

Blackcurrant mousse is topped with a quenelle of Italian meringue and drizzled with sugar syrup. A sugar wafer is supported between two pieces of orange, garnished with pomegranate seeds. A diagonal line of sugar sand is used as a graphic on the plate.

1 Prepare the sugar syrup base as shown on page 134. Line a baking sheet with a piece of parchment paper. Have the large bowl of iced water ready.

2 Heat the syrup to the caramel stage, then plunge the pan into iced water to stop it cooking further. Do not leave it in the iced water; you need the syrup to remain liquid for the next stage.

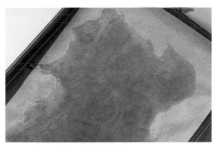

3 Quickly pour the syrup onto the lined baking sheet. You shouldn't need all of the caramel mix because the depth of the sheet will be relatively thin. Instead, move and tilt the sheet to spread out the syrup, keeping it as thin as possible. Set aside to cool and harden.

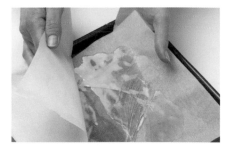

4 Once cooled, you can start to break it into wafers. Your fingers will leave an imprint on the hardened caramel and take the shine off the surface, so place your hands over and under the parchment paper, as shown. Make a single tap to break the caramel into wafers. When ready to serve, pick out desired wafers for use.

Sugar shards

- Sugar syrup base (see page 134)
- Heavy pan (a copper pan is ideal)
- Pastry brush
- Sugar thermometer
- Baking sheet
- Parchment paper

PRESENTATION

Sugar shards are presented attractively on top of two ice-cream quenelles, served on a path of toasted almonds.

→**TIP**

- These sugar shards can be kept for about three days under normal circumstances, but in humid conditions make them as close to serving as possible to avoid softening. The sugar will absorb any moisture that's in the air, so store in an airtight container until serving.

Shards of hardened caramel can be used for a dramatic presentation – especially if positioned upright so that the light glints off the surfaces. For added interest, try flavouring the caramel with raspberry syrup.

1 Prepare the caramel syrup as shown on page 134. Line a baking sheet with parchment paper. When the syrup has reached the caramel stage, take the pan in one hand using an oven glove and hold the lined baking sheet in the other hand, resting it on your work surface.

2 Pour the syrup out onto the lined baking sheet, tilting and moving as you do so to spread it around the space evenly. It should have a thickness of 2 to 3 mm (1/8 in). Set the caramel aside to cool and harden for about 30 minutes.

3 When the caramel is quite hard, pull the parchment paper away from the sheet. If you leave the paper attached, your shards will not be as impressive.

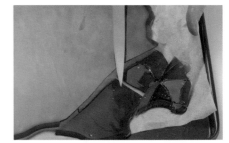

4 Gently slide your hand under the parchment paper, supporting the sheet of caramel, and taking care not to touch it or leave any marks. Use the tip of a knife to sharply tap on the sheet near one end, which will cause it to shatter into attractive shards. Repeat at the other end. Insert your shards upright into cream or ice cream.

Sugar sticks and twists

YOU WILL NEED

- Sugar syrup base (see page 134)
- Heavy pan (a copper pan is ideal)
- Pastry brush
- Sugar thermometer
- Baking sheet
- Parchment paper
- Two forks

PRESENTATION

A ball of raspberry ice cream, dashes of raspberry coulis and fresh raspberries are presented on a line of walnut agrodolce, with a dramatic top note of a sugar stick.

→TIPS

- You will have to work quickly since the syrup cools to an unworkable temperature very rapidly.
- Make sure you serve these sugar garnishes on the same day.

These garnishes require impeccable timing and patience – the temperature of the sugar has to be just right. If you have enough equipment, it's wise to make two batches of sugar so that you can be working on one while the other heats up to the correct temperature.

1 Make a caramel syrup as shown on page 134. Line a baking sheet with parchment paper. Set the sugar pan at an angle on a folded towel to hold it in place and to retain the temperature for a little longer. Use two forks to lift a little of the syrup; twist the forks to lift up the strands.

2 Lift the two forks with the syrup over to a corner of the baking sheet, keeping the syrup contained within a small area.

3 Disentangle one of the forks, and set it aside. Hold the baking sheet steady with one hand, and scoop some syrup onto the other fork.

4 Now gently but firmly pull away with the fork, to a height of 25 cm (10 in) or so, leaving in the wake of the fork a strand of sugar that will harden almost instantly. Break off and neaten the end of the strand. To make the sugar stick into a sugar spiral, twist the strand around as you pull away with the fork.

Sugar sand

This clever but simple sugar decoration can be used in a variety of stylistic ways. For added plate appeal, use sugar sand for visual interest or to give texture to a dish.

✔ YOU WILL NEED

- Sugar syrup base (see page 134)
- Heavy pan (a copper pan is ideal)
- Pastry brush
- Sugar thermometer
- Baking sheet
- Parchment paper
- Large bowl of iced water

PRESENTATION

Sugar sand is sprinkled on the plate for visual interest. It is topped with a raspberry mousse and decorated with chopped pistachios. The plate is finished with a few fresh raspberries and mint leaves.

→ TIP

- The sugar sand will keep for up to a week, depending on humidity, in an airtight container. You will need to break it up a little after storage.

1 Make the sugar syrup base as directed on page 134. Line a baking sheet with parchment paper.

2 Heat the syrup to the caramel stage, and immediately plunge the base of the pan into a bowl of iced water to stop it cooking further. If it goes past this stage it will burn and the batch will have to be discarded, so be careful.

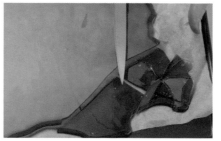

3 Pour the caramel syrup onto the lined baking sheet, allowing it to spread naturally. Set aside to cool and harden for about 30 minutes. Break into rough shards using the tip of a knife.

4 Transfer the sugar shards to a food processor, and process until broken into fine crystals. If you don't have a food processor, make an envelope out of parchment paper and put the shards inside. Now bash the envelope sharply with a hammer or similar utensil to create the sand. Your sand is now ready for sprinkling.

Sugar plate decoration

Sugar syrup can be used to stunning effect, straight from the pan. With this freer way of presenting, you can really get creative with your plate decoration and add a sweet base to your dessert at the same time.

✔ YOU WILL NEED

- Sugar syrup base (see page 134)
- Pastry brush
- Heavy pan (a copper pan is ideal)
- Sugar thermometer
- Large bowl of iced water

PRESENTATION

A chocolate larieux (mousse au chocolat) is presented on a plate decorated with a simple circular line of caramel syrup and sprinkled with sugar sand, while the accompanying quenelle of cream is decorated with a shard of caramel.

→ TIPS

- The plates can be prepared up to an hour in advance with the sugar plate decoration, and then stored until ready to use.

1 Make the sugar syrup as directed on page 134. Have a bowl of iced water ready.

2 Heat to caramel stage, and plunge the base of the pan into the bowl of iced water to prevent it cooking any further.

3 Have ready the plates that you wish to decorate. Set the sugar pan at an angle, on a folded kitchen towel to hold it in place – the bulk of the syrup will help to retain the temperature for a little longer.

4 Working quickly, use a teaspoon to drizzle the caramel syrup attractively on the plate in your chosen design. A circular design is shown above, for a zigzag alternative, see page 134.

Sugar baskets

The irregular ends of these delicate sugar baskets give them a dramatic flair that will certainly be a hit with your guests, but they do require an experienced hand. For the best results, make and serve on the same day.

✔ YOU WILL NEED

- Sugar syrup base (see page 134)
- Heavy pan (a copper pan is ideal)
- Pastry brush
- Large bowl of iced water
- Sugar thermometer
- Preparation tray
- Parchment paper cut into 10 cm (4 in) squares
- Mini muffin paper cups
- Toothpick
- Teaspoon

1 Make the sugar syrup as directed on page 134. Have a bowl of iced water ready.

2 Heat to caramel stage, and plunge the base of the pan into the bowl of iced water to prevent the syrup cooking any further.

→ TIPS

- The basket edges can be easily tidied up by breaking and smoothing off the unwanted points with a little water and a paintbrush.
- If you prefer an even more dramatic look, set the mini muffin paper cups over a cork or similar prop to hold them further from the surface, and drizzle the syrup over. The points of the drizzles will extend upon drying.

3 On a preparation tray, set out four or five parchment paper squares. Put the mini muffin paper cups upside down on top of the squares. This set-up will make it easier to manoeuvre the basket as you drizzle the syrup.

4 Set the sugar pan at an angle on a folded kitchen towel to hold it in place, so that the bulk of the syrup will help to retain the temperature for a little longer. Steady the muffin cup with a toothpick and, working quickly but gently, pour a teaspoon of syrup over to cover the base.

A sugar basket is filled with white chocolate ice cream rolled in almonds, and presented on top of an explosion of cocoa, served with fresh raspberries and mango.
To create an explosion of cocoa powder, drop a small amount onto the centre of the plate and blow on it gently with a straw.

5 Turn the mini muffin baskets by holding a corner of the parchment paper square. Continue to spoon the syrup over the bases of the paper cups, allowing it to cascade down the sides. Use a circular movement to spread the syrup and encourage it down the sides in drizzles. If too much syrup is used in each pour, the drizzles will end in unattractive pools.

6 Set aside to cool and harden for about 20 minutes. Handle the baskets very gently to avoid breakages. Upturn the baskets in the palm of your hand, and gently pull the paper cups away from the baskets. Fill your baskets with your chosen filling and serve.

Sugar cage

A sugar cage is a firm favourite with pastry chefs; the dramatic presentation showcases an advanced level of skill. The beading on this sugar cage adds a jewel-like quality. For best results, serve on the same day.

- Sugar syrup base (see page 134)
- Heavy pan (a copper pan is ideal)
- Pastry brush
- Sugar thermometer
- Large bowl of iced water
- Soup ladle or utensil with a similar shape to act as a mould
- Oil for greasing
- Preparation tray
- Two teaspoons

1 Make the syrup as directed on page 134, Have a bowl of iced water ready. When it reaches caramel stage, plunge the base of the pan into the iced water immediately to stop the syrup cooking any further.

2 Set the sugar pan at an angle on a folded kitchen towel so that it's held securely in place on your work surface. The bulk of the syrup will help to retain the temperature for a little longer. Lightly oil the outside of a soup ladle so that the sugar cage does not stick.

→TIPS

- To achieve the sugar cage with success, careful preparation is required. Ensure that you won't be interrupted and that everything is in place before you start. You will need to work with speed but not haste, and you may need to reheat the syrup once or twice. The syrup will not reheat more than twice, so if you need to, make another batch of caramel to finish off the cage.
- Removing the cage from the ladle can be tricky, so do this as soon as it is cool and store until use, instead of rushing the task at serving time.

3 Position the preparation tray underneath the ladle to catch the drips. Take the ladle in one hand, and with a teaspoon in the other, pick up a little syrup. Use the spoon to drizzle syrup over the back of the ladle.

4 Continue picking up syrup and drizzling lines in one direction across the ladle, allowing the drips to fall onto the tray. Cover the entire surface of the ladle.

PRESENTATION

Strawberry ice cream is presented inside a sugar cage and served alongside fresh strawberries and a drizzle of mango sauce.

5 Next, holding two teaspoons in one hand, pick up some more syrup. Twist the ladle around and drizzle lines of syrup at right angles to the first set of drizzles. You may find it easier to hold the ladle in one place and move the teaspoons around the ladle instead.

6 Make sure that there is an even covering over the ladle, so that it holds together. Hook the ladle over the edge of a shelf or work surface and allow the caramel to cool and harden. Once hard, gently prise the sugar cage from the ladle, making sure there are no drips over the edge of the spoon, holding the cage on. Fix any holes or breakages by drizzling a little more syrup.

Chocolate garnishes

Creating chocolate decorations is an opportunity to show off the skill and mastery of the cook. Chocolate lends itself well to finishes and decorations, since it can be melted to a silky, flowing consistency and is ideal for dipping and spreading out to paper-thin sheets. When it sets solidly, chocolate scrapes into curls and frills quite easily. Chocolate is a challenge to work with, however, since it can separate during cooking. The purest chocolate has the higher proportion of solids, and is therefore more stable and easier to work with. Testament to the skill of a professional patissier is the mastery of a white-chocolate creation, because white chocolate has no cocoa solids, making it even more difficult to work with.

Preparing chocolate

Chocolatiers, individuals who are skilled in the art of working with chocolate, work hard to avoid having this valuable commodity 'seize'. Seizing occurs when the chocolate separates into cocoa fats and cocoa solids, and it is a chocolatier's worst nightmare. Chocolate must be discarded if this occurs.

Although chocolate manufactured for home use has been made easier to handle, it does need careful attention – this unstable ingredient can be the source of much stress in the kitchen.

The chocolate may seize for a variety of reasons, including sudden changes in temperature and the presence of small droplets of water, steam, foreign bodies or grease in the chocolate. Over-stirring can also cause the chocolate to separate.

There are some useful rules to follow when working with chocolate. Give yourself plenty of time to create your chocolate decoration, and do it before you prepare the other components of the meal. Chocolate absorbs flavours quite readily, and can therefore be easily tainted with the wrong flavours.

For all of the decorations in this chapter, the chocolate is first melted. Avoid preparing too much chocolate at once, so you have enough left if it is required again later in the recipe. For example, the recipe for chocolate cups (see pages 148–149) requires two coats of painted chocolate. It's better to heat half first and then heat the rest after you've applied the first coat. Below is a step-by-step guide to melting chocolate.

1 Before you melt your chocolate, break it up into squares. If you want it to melt faster, grate it. Put the chocolate into a ceramic or Pyrex bowl that's slightly bigger than your saucepan. Don't use a metallic bowl because this will heat up the chocolate too quickly and cause it to spoil. It may be easier to use a plate at this stage.

2 If you are adding another ingredient to the chocolate, do so at this stage so that you can melt and mix them together. Cream is the most common ingredient to mix with chocolate. If you

add ingredients later in the melting process, it may cause the chocolate to seize due to the sudden change in temperature. Make sure you judge when to add other ingredients wisely.

3 Set the bowl over a pan of simmering water. To prevent the chocolate becoming too hot, it is important that the bowl does not touch the water. It is also important that the bowl fits snugly over the pan to prevent the condensation from steam spoiling the chocolate.

4 Heat the chocolate until melted, but do not let the water boil or the chocolate will become too hot. It will also create steam, and the water droplets this creates will cause the chocolate to seize. If you need to stir the chocolate, move the bowl around first to agitate the contents. If that doesn't work, stir the chocolate slowly with a fork.

5 If the chocolate is to be cooled, set it aside to cool slowly. Do not dip the bowl in iced water, as the sudden change in temperature will cause the chocolate to seize.

Chocolate squares

Chocolate can be easily turned into the form of a sheet and shaped in a number of different ways. Below is the method for squares. Use these elegant decorations to adorn chocolate mousse, or tarte au chocolat.

PRESENTATION

Vanilla and white-chocolate ice cream is decorated with gold leaf chocolate squares and served with a drizzle of chocolate. Accompanying it are mango and berries dusted with cocoa.

→TIP

- These simple chocolate decorations are actually quite versatile. They can be used flat, as a base, stacked with a mousse or cream filling or used upright as shown above. If decorating a tart, arrange in the centre in a neat circle.

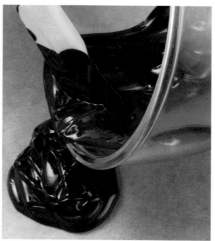

1 Melt a batch of chocolate as directed on page 145. To make six decorations you will need just over 50 g (1½ oz) of chocolate. Line a baking sheet with parchment paper and pour the chocolate out to an even thickness.

2 Working quickly, use a stepped palette knife to spread the chocolate into a thin sheet. You are aiming for a thickness of just under 1 to 2 mm (⅛ in). Set aside to cool and harden. Do not refrigerate

1 To add gold leaf decoration to the squares, leave the edible gold leaf on the backing paper, and use a small, sharp knife to cut it into strips. Set out the chocolate squares on a kitchen plate or preparation tray, and position the gold leaf next to them. Now cut the strips into squares for the chocolate squares. Of course, size will depend on your personal preference.

3 Just before the chocolate hardens completely, use a small sharp knife to score the surface and divide it into six even squares (or more if you prefer). Do not use a ruler for guidance since it will mark the chocolate. It is easier to get straight lines with a quick movement of the knife, so use the edge of the baking sheet as your guide.

4 Set the chocolate aside until it sets completely. This should take about 15 minutes. When quite cool, use an artist's palette knife to separate the squares. Insert into your chosen dessert and serve. You can store the squares for up to three days in an airtight container.

2 Use a medium-sized paintbrush to lift the gold leaf from the backing paper and onto the chocolate squares. Use a toothpick to help you position the delicate square of gold leaf. The gold leaf will naturally adhere to the chocolate, and then your squares will be ready to serve.

Chocolate cups

This is a very sweet presentation designed to impress. The cups can be paired with many flavours and differing textures. Chocolate presented in this way also adds another texture to your dessert plate.

→ **TIP**

- For added drama, use white chocolate to paint on the second layer of the chocolate cup, or vice versa, and the layers will show up as contrasting brown and white.

1 Melt a batch of chocolate as directed on page 145. Make sure that the muffin cups are very clean and dry. Dust or grease will cause the chocolate to bloom unattractively.

2 Use a paintbrush to coat the inside of the muffin cup with chocolate, making sure that you reach into the pleats, and that there are no air holes. Paint right up to the top of the paper's edge, but not over it. This attention to detail will give the best finish.

3 Melt a second batch of chocolate and paint a second coat over the first coat. Paint all the way up to the edge, to make a solid line that will look neat when removed from the cups, but more importantly, will not break during this process.

4 Set the mini muffin cups aside to cool and harden. Do not refrigerate, but leave in a cool, dry place. A dark larder is ideal, or a on a marble or granite block.

5 To unmould the cups, hold them very lightly and use a toothpick to gently prise the paper away from the chocolate. Gently work the toothpick all around the cup.

6 Turn the cup upside down onto a plate and lift away the paper. When handling the cups, be sure to do so with care, to avoid any breakages. The cups can be stored in an airtight container for up to seven days. Serve with your preferred filling and dust with cocoa powder to finish.

PRESENTATION

This simple chocolate cup has been used to add richness, texture and form to a fruit dessert of raspberries, mango slivers and pineapple wafers.

Chocolate flakes

YOU WILL NEED

- Melted chocolate (see page 145)
- Small cube mould or similar
- Metal spatula

PRESENTATION

Vanilla ice cream is balled and presented with a pineapple wafer divider and accompanied by mango purée. The pale colour scheme is set off with a dramatic sprinkling of dark chocolate flakes, also adding texture and flavour.

→TIPS

- Keep the cube of melted and moulded chocolate wrapped in a cool, dark place so that you always have chocolate flakes ready to decorate desserts when required.

Chocolate flakes are easy to create, and yet, sprinkled over a dessert make for a stunning presentation. The beauty is in the irregularity of the flake, so do not try too hard to make each one the same size.

1 First melt the chocolate as instructed on page 145. Take care not to overheat.

2 Pour the chocolate into the cube mould. Set aside to cool and harden for about 30 minutes.

3 At the end of this time, tap the mould to release the chocolate. If this proves difficult, immerse the mould very briefly in boiling water to loosen. Then tap the chocolate free.

4 Set the chocolate block on a chopping board and use a metal spatula to scrape down the face of the block and flake the chocolate. Sprinkle the flakes over your preferred dessert.

Chocolate leaves

This classic decoration for a fruit-based dessert is a neat way of bridging the gap between orchard and plate. The cork and pin technique can be used in other applications where delicate handling is required.

- Melted chocolate (see page 145)
- Six small, fresh fruit tree leaves
- Parchment paper
- Scissors
- Cork
- Pins
- Paintbrush
- Preparation tray
- Tweezers

PRESENTATION

A simple line of chocolate is piped in a circular pattern, topped with apple galette on puff pastry, and decorated with dredged chocolate leaves.

→TIP

- If your chocolate leaf cracks as you separate it from the fresh leaf, carry on and remove the leaf while trying to minimize cracks. Set the leaf down on the paper square, and paint over the crack on the messy side of the leaf with a little melted chocolate.

1 Melt the chocolate over a pan of water as as instructed on page 145. Next cut 12 squares of parchment paper just bigger than the fruit leaves.

2 Take a cork and top it with a paper square and one of the leaves. Secure with a pin. This will make the handling of the leaf much easier while you paint, and you can turn it as needed.

3 Pick up the cork, and use a paintbrush to brush the melted chocolate onto the leaf. Make sure that the chocolate goes into the veins and crevices. Turn the painted leaf onto a clean paper square set on the preparation tray. Paint all leaves. Set aside to harden for about 20 minutes. Paint another layer of chocolate onto the leaves.

4 Once hardened, take the paper square that the leaf is set on, and holding one end of the fresh leaf with tweezers, pull away from the chocolate leaf slowly and gently. The imprint of the fine veins and crevices will be revealed. This will be the good side of the leaf, and the side to present on your plate for your final presentation.

Chocolate flowers

This three-dimensional decoration is the perfect opportunity for you to show off your piping skills. To create the flowers, use a ribbon piping nozzle – it has an opening shaped like a very flat almond.

YOU WILL NEED

- 100 g (3¹/₂ oz) chocolate
- 100 ml (3¹/₃ fl oz) double cream
- Non-metallic bowl
- Cling film
- Electric whisk
- Piping bag
- Ribbon piping nozzle

PRESENTATION

Three chocolate flowers piped asymmetrically on the plate are served with drizzled raspberry coulis and berries, clustered and dusted with icing sugar. It's topped off with a delicate chocolate wafer and a mint leaf.

→TIP

- For extra drama in your presentation, vary the size of the flower. A small, medium and large one across the middle of the plate creates a great effect, especially when used together with chocolate leaves (see page 151).

1 Mix together the cream and chocolate in a non-metallic bowl set over a pan of simmering water. Melt and mix the ingredients together as instructed on page 145.

2 Cover the bowl with cling film, then refrigerate for at least two hours or overnight.

3 When the chocolate and cream mixture is quite cold, beat with an electric whisk until the mixture has doubled in volume and becomes thick. This will take 5–10 minutes. Fit the piping bag with the ribbon nozzle. Spoon the chocolate ganache into the piping bag.

4 To pipe a six-petal flower, hold the nozzle upright against the plate. Start at the centre and pipe a petal, moving the bag back and forth slightly to give a rippled effect. Finish by twisting the nozzle into the plate. Repeat with the remaining petals. Refrigerate until required.

Chocolate piping

- Melted chocolate (see page 145)
- Pencil
- Letter paper
- Parchment paper
- Piping bag
- Small circular piping nozzle
- Stepped palette knife

PRESENTATION

This plate has been lined with sugar sand and a swipe of butterscotch sauce, then topped with balls of vanilla ice cream and chocolate piped decorations.

→TIP

- Practise piping initials. Your guests will be thrilled with a plate personalized with their initials in delicious piped chocolate.

Piped chocolate designs can be many and varied. The key to success is to ensure that the chocolate is of the right consistency to pipe. Test a little on a separate piece of paper before you begin.

1 Melt the chocolate over a pan of water as instructed on page 145.

2 Meanwhile, draw your desired designs in pencil on a white letter-sized sheet of paper. Use more than one sheet if needed. Cover this with a sheet of parchment paper of the same size.

3 Fit the nozzle onto the piping bag, and spoon the melted chocolate into the bag. Using your drawn designs as a guide, pipe the chocolate onto the parchment paper. When you are finished, tidy up the ends with the help of a toothpick. Set aside to cool and harden.

4 To remove the designs from the parchment paper, use a stepped palette knife to gently prise it from the bottom of the finished designs. These chocolate piped designs can be stored in a sealed airtight container for up to one week. Use to adorn your guests' desserts.

USEFUL INFORMATION

In the pages that follow, you'll find a range of information to aid you in your food presentation. Here you'll find seasonality and culinary uses for a range of edible flowers, shoots and leaves, core recipes referenced in The Technique Directory, a kitchen schedule to help you plan and prepare a menu and a handy weights and measures conversion chart.

Edible flowers (savoury)

Violets and nasturtiums were considered 'salad herbs' as far back as the 15th century, and they are still frequently used to enhance salads and appetizers, adding colour and zest. But there are many others that can be used in cooking. The following are recommended for salads and savoury entrées. Use flowers sparingly and note that they are not suitable for those who suffer allergic reactions or suffer from asthma.

Nasturtiums *Tropaeolum majus*
Ranging in colour from a brick red to bright yellow, the petals of the nasturtium flower have a pleasantly strong peppery flavour.

Season:	Summer
Uses:	The bright colours will dress up a savoury plate and give a welcome kick to a green salad. They can also be used to flavour butter, cream cheese and vinegars.

Calendula *Asteraceae officinalis*
A bright and tasty addition to salads, often used to bring colour to a dish, although their aroma is not sweet and resembles the scent of hops in beer.

Season:	Summer
Uses:	Use the yellow petals as an economical substitute for saffron and to add subtle flavour to seafood and soups.

Bergamot *Citrus bergamia*
A fragrant plant that has a variety of uses for both its leaves and petals.

Season:	Late spring to summer
Uses:	Mixed with nasturtium and calendula, its lightly fragranced petals will make a good salad to accompany savouries. Bergamot leaves can also be dried to make tea, most commonly Earl Grey.

French marigold *Tagetes patula*
The petals of the French marigold are a lovely golden yellow in hue, with a citric taste.

Season:	Summer
Uses:	The petals taste of orange and lemon. Use in sandwiches, salads and seafood chowders. These flowers will also work well in hot desserts.

Pansies *Viola*

This garden flower has a mild flavour that moves from slightly sweet to sharp. It can also be used as a sweet garnish (see page 158).

Season: From late spring to mid summer
Uses: Similar to nasturtiums but with a less peppery taste, the bright petals of this flower are ideal for livening up green salads.

Sorrel *Rumex acetosa*

The sharpness of taste makes sorrel a good stand-in for fruit in off-seasons, with meat dishes.

Season: May–August
Uses: Sorrel adds a lemony flavour to salads. Finely chop
the leaves and combine with olive oil to create a green citric sauce for fish.

Tagetes *Compositae erecta lemmonii*

Another flower which provides a hint of citrus aroma to dishes.

Season: Summer
Uses: The petals' hint of lemon make tagetes ideal for use with seafood.

Rosemary *Rosmarinus officinalis*

The delicate flowers of the rosemary plant have an aromatic flavour that is less intense than the leaves.

Season: Spring
Uses: A great addition to savoury dishes, rosemary works particularly well with red meat such as lamb.

Cornflower *Centaurea montana*

These beautiful blue flowers have a strong, clove-like taste.

Season: Summer
Uses: Ideal for use on savoury dishes that will benefit from a bright, bold garnish, but use sparingly.

Basil flowers *Ocimum basilicum*

Flowers can be pale pink, white or a delicate lavender. The flowers have a similar taste to the leaves of the plant, but are much milder, and can sometimes possess a slight lemon or mint taste.

Season: Summer (but you can control this by pinching out the flowers and allowing them to bloom when required).
Uses: Providing they aren't too bitter, basil flowers are great in salads, soups and pastas, or as a pretty plate garnish.

Edible flowers (sweet)

Flowers are a pretty addition to any dish but particularly appropriate to sweet dishes. Many can be easily grown in the garden – please don't pick wild ones. Although strictly seasonal, they can be preserved for use at a later date, so you can make use of them throughout the year. The following flowers are recommended for crystallization and sweet dishes.

Borage *Borago officinalis*
The bright blue flower of the borage plant with its purple stamens has a crisp, refreshing taste.
Season: May–September
Uses: Borage makes a fragrant addition to summer desserts and is ideal for using in ice bowls.

Primroses *Primula vulgaris*
A sweet-tasting flower with scented overtones. Avoid picking wild primroses.
Season: March–May
Uses: Ideal for use as decoration on desserts or candied as the petals provide a good structure. The sweetness of primroses lends itself to making wine or vinaigrette and you can also crystallize them and use in pancakes.

Pansies *Viola*
The sweetness of the pansy petal with its sharp overtones is an ideal choice for candying since the sharpness balances the candy. It also gives a structure to the work.
Season: Late spring to early summer
Uses: Candy and use to top desserts such as jellies and cakes.

Violets *Viola odorata*
The sweetness of the petals is highly scented and lends itself well to being candied and used extensively for decorative work.
Season: March–May
Uses: Can be candied to top desserts and delicate ices, or added with almonds to rice pudding. Violets can also be used as a sweet dressing for meats such as veal, or used in soup.

Pinks *Caryophyllaceae*
A common garden flower that has surprisingly spicy overtones.

Season:	May–June
Uses:	Although it may be used for savoury dishes, this flower is ideal for candied work. Its strong, spicy flavour, reminiscent of cloves, makes it perfect for adding to jams and sweet-sour pickles.

Dog rose *Rosa canina*
This rose has a slightly lighter fragrance than many garden roses. The fruity flavour will improve both fruit dishes and summer drinks.

Season:	August–November
Uses:	The delicate flavour can give sweet overtones to a salad and is commonly used for sugaring. It also works well with coconut, honey or added to vinegar.

Lavender *Lavandula angustifolia*
Often used in cake decorations since the cluster of blue flowers makes a good structure and has a great aroma

Season:	Summer
Uses:	Make lavender sugar for desserts. Also works well as an infusion for sauces and syrups.

Sweet William *Dianthus barbatus*
The petals of this flower have a sweet zesty flavour with lemon overtones.

Season:	June–July
Uses:	Good for adding a sweet zest to ice cream, sorbets, salads, fruit salad, dessert sauces and even stir-fries.

Cowslip *Primula veris*
The leaves can be used as a salad green, although the bright petals have a sweet-scented flavour, ideal for sweet dishes.

Season:	Spring
Uses:	The large petals lend themselves to being candied or for mixing with chocolate. They can also be used in making sweet vinaigrette.

Nasturtiums *Tropaeolum majus*
Ranging in colour from a brick red to bright yellow, the petals of the nasturtium flower have a pleasantly strong peppery flavour.

Season:	Summer
Uses:	These flowers can be used in savoury dishes (see page 156), but their pungency is also ideal for adding to sweet dishes such as sharp apple sorbet, or for combining with sweet, soft cheeses.

Edible shoots and leaves

A healthy dose of imagination is vital when cooking. Styling your food to whet the appetite and inspire the diner is obviously crucial, but occasionally including an unusual ingredient is another way to bring an element of surprise to the table. Below is a short list of shoots. Use them with care and restraint for a simple but delicious accompaniment to your meal.

Dandelion shoots *Taraxacum species*
With strong peppery overtones, dandelion shoots make a tasty salad plant. Collect the leaves only when they are young.

Season:	April–May
Uses:	Roughly chopped they are a great addition to a salad and work well with a trace of garlic.

Wild asparagus *Asparagus officinalis*
A familiar taste is given an extra zestful edge when using the wild species.

Season:	May–August
Uses:	Take the spears that grow from the shoot, but be careful not to take the root. The strong taste of the asparagus is accompanied well with salted foods.

Broad-bean tops *Vicia faba*
Often neglected, broad-bean tops are a valuable source as an alternative spring green.

Season:	Spring
Uses:	A wonderful treat for the greedy gardener, broad-bean tops are great with risotto, or wilted with butter.

Pea shoots *Pisum sativum*
This is becoming an increasingly popular early-summer salad vegetable.

Season:	May–June
Uses:	Cut early and it can be eaten raw as an alternative salad. The shoots have a light peppery taste that works well as a background salad.

Stinging-nettle leaf shoots *Urtica dioica*

Similar in taste, these shoots make a good alternative to spinach. They are also high in vitamins.

Season:	Pick before June (in high summer the leaves become bitter and can act as a laxative).
Uses:	Young shoots have a strong 'iron'-like taste that works well with leeks, cabbage and bacon or lardons.

Wild rocket *Diplotaxis tenuifolia*

The peppery, hazelnut taste of rocket livens up a salad bowl and is a useful green to have year-round.

Season:	Year-round.
Uses:	Rocket works well on its own with simple dressing. Its spiky taste is also ideal as an alternative to basil in pesto.

Hawthorn leaf shoots *Crataegus monogyna*

The young leaves have a pleasant nutty taste.

Season:	April
Uses:	The leaves are a good alternative to spring greens and an ideal accompaniment to strong cheese. Chop with sorrel and garlic and use as a dressing for red meats. The leaves also blend well with potato.

Chickweed *Stellaria media*

A savoury taste that is reminiscent of lettuce.

Season:	January–February
Uses:	Ideal as part of a winter salad, chickweed also mixes well with the peppery taste of watercress. Use as a garnish for savoury dishes.

Samphire *Salicornia species*

A crisp, tangy salad vegetable that has a refreshing taste with light citrus overtones and saltiness.

Season:	June–July
Uses:	Samphire lends itself to being treated in a similar way to asparagus, and is best served with melted butter, or as an accompaniment to fish and poultry.

Hop shoots *Humulus lupulus*

Hop shoots have a strong, sharp taste that goes well with butter and eggs.

Season:	Pick the shoots before May.
Uses:	In Italy, hop shoots are popular when used in a frittata in the same way that asparagus might be. The strong taste can be balanced by the blandness of eggs or butter, but also complements strong, salty cheeses such as Parmesan.

Recipes

In this section, you'll find a range of generic recipes that are referenced within The Technique Directory. You may find it useful to cross refer to the weights and measures information given on page 170.

SWEET PASTRY

The success of your pastry decorations depends on the quality of the flour you use. Using a better brand of flour not only makes it easier to roll the dough, but it also gives a silkier looking finish to your pastry. Use this pastry to make lattice (page 48), sails (page 49), hoops (page 50) or baskets and cups (page 51).

Makes
Makes 6 tart cases, or 250 g (8³/4 oz) pastry

Time

✔ **YOU WILL NEED**

- 150 g (5¹/₂ oz) good-quality all-purpose flour
- 1 tablespoon sifted icing sugar
- Pinch of salt
- 75 g (2 oz) chilled unsalted butter, diced
- 2 tablespoons iced water

TUILE PASTE

This delicate paste mixture can be moulded into a number of different shapes to form a variety of garnishes (see pages 52–53). If you like, flavour the tuiles with a little coffee powder, food essence or similar, before adding the egg whites.

Makes
12

Time

✔ **YOU WILL NEED**

- 50 g (1¹/₄ oz) softened unsalted butter
- 50 g (1¹/₄ oz) superfine sugar
- 50 g (1¹/₄ oz) liquid glucose
- 50 g (1¹/₄ oz) all-purpose flour

CARROT JELLY

This unexpectedly savoury jelly can be presented in balls, cubes or other forms (depending on the mould used), and makes a nice counterpoint in texture and flavour to traditional dishes.

Makes
500 ml (17 fl oz)

Time

✔ **YOU WILL NEED**

- 750 g (26 oz) carrots, peeled
- 3 sheets gelatine, soaked in cold water to soften

VEGETABLE PURÉE

This simple vegetable purée is the basis of many other presentations. The steaming preserves the colour, texture and flavour.

Makes
750 g (26 oz) of purée serves 8–10

Time

✔ **YOU WILL NEED**

- 600 g (21 oz) of beetroot, carrot or alternative vegetable
- 150 g (5 oz) caster sugar

METHOD

Food processor method

To make your pastry in a food processor, blend together the flour, icing sugar and salt, and gradually add the diced butter. Add the water slowly to the mix, and as soon as the pastry comes together, turn off the food processor.

By hand

To make your pastry by hand, stir together the flour, icing sugar and salt. Add the butter and use a rubbing and lifting motion between your thumbs and forefingers to mix in the butter and achieve a breadcrumb-like consistency. Stir in the water, teaspoon by teaspoon, until the dough comes together.

Then

Wrap in parchment paper. Chill until ready to use, but for at least 30 minutes. Proceed according to your pastry decoration method. Bake pastry decorations at 200°C (400°F). Cool on a wire rack.

 METHOD

1 Beat together the butter and sugar until pale and creamy.
2 Stir in the liquid glucose and flour. Cover and refrigerate until ready to use.

3 Proceed as directed on pages 52–53.
4 Bake at 190°C (375°F) for 5 minutes or so.

METHOD

1 Dice the carrots. Steam them over boiling water for 10 minutes, or until they are tender. Alternatively, simmer in boiling water until just cooked. Do not overcook them or they will lose their colour.

2 Purée the carrots in a food processor, or using a stick blender.
3 Line a bowl with cheesecloth, and spoon the purée into the centre. Twist up the mixture inside the cheesecloth and squeeze

out the carrot juice into the bowl, until the purée is quite dry.
4 Pour the juice into a pan and heat gently. Add the gelatine and stir until dissolved. Pour into mould to set (see pages 56–57)

METHOD

1 Peel and dice the vegetables. Steam for about 10 minutes or until tender.
2 While still hot, blend with the sugar using a hand blender or food processor until fine.
3 Proceed as shown in recipe.

MUSTARD SAUCE

This is a very versatile sauce on which to present lamb, beef or pork dishes. It also complements well-seasoned fish, chicken and poultry dishes.

Serves
4

Time

YOU WILL NEED

- 2 shallots, sliced
- 3 garlic cloves
- 30 g (1 oz) butter
- 2 teaspoons white wine vinegar
- 1 bay leaf, 2 sprigs thyme
- 200 ml (7 fl oz) vegetable stock
- Salt and black pepper
- 2 tablespoons mustard

RED BELL PEPPER SAUCE

The red colour of this sauce makes a wonderful base when the main component of a dish is a paler colour, for example, fish or chicken. It is also successful as a swipe, or spotted to garnish a contemporary presentation.

Serves
4

Time

YOU WILL NEED

- 2 red bell peppers
- 2 shallots, sliced
- 3 garlic cloves
- 1 teaspoon fennel seeds
- 2 tablespoons olive oil
- 1 tablespoon white wine vinegar, salt and pepper
- 200 ml (7 fl oz) vegetable stock
- 30 g (1 oz) butter

VEGETABLE SORBET

The savoury flavour of this sorbet is unexpected and quite versatile. It is especially successful when used with a savoury jelly, and contrasting colours and textures. Because raw egg white is used, discard after 5 days.

Serves
10–12 as a garnish

Time

YOU WILL NEED

- 750 g (26 oz) carrots
- Pinch of sugar
- Sea salt
- 1 egg white

CREAMED POTATO

Creamed potato should have a very fine and smooth texture – many chefs would sieve after mashing to refine the texture. It is important to use the correct floury potatoes.

Serves
4

Time

YOU WILL NEED

- 800 g (28 oz) floury potatoes for mashing
- Salt and black pepper
- 100 g (3½ oz) butter

SAVOURY MERINGUE

This meringue recipe holds a subtle savoury flavour, in a delicate texture. The meringue works well when served with jelly or sorbet in a savoury context, for a melange of vegetables.

Makes
Approximately 20 tablespoons of meringue

Time

YOU WILL NEED

- 500 g (18 oz) beetroot, peeled and diced
- Pinch of sugar
- Sea salt
- 3 x 8 g (⅕ oz) sachets dried egg white

STOCK SYRUP

Stock syrup is made from equal quantities of sugar and water, so 100 g (3½ oz) sugar, for instance, would need 100 ml (3½ fl oz) water. This stock syrup is used in all recipes on pages 134–143.

Makes
As required

Time

YOU WILL NEED

- Sugar
- Water
(Choose amounts suitable to your recipe)

🍴 METHOD

1 Sauté the shallots and garlic in the butter over medium heat for 10 minutes until soft.
2 Add the vinegar to the pan, followed by the bay leaf, thyme and stock. Season with salt and pepper. Simmer for 15 minutes over medium heat. Drain through a very fine sieve and set the juice to one side.
3 To serve, heat through the juice over medium heat, and whisk in the mustard.

🍴 METHOD

1 Chop and seed the peppers, then sauté with the shallots, garlic and fennel seeds in the olive oil over medium heat for 10 minutes until softened.
2 Pour on the vinegar, then the stock. Season with salt and pepper. Simmer for 15 minutes over medium heat. Drain the mixture through a very fine sieve. Set aside the liquid until ready to serve.
3 To serve, reheat the liquid over medium heat, and beat in the butter.

🍴 METHOD

1 Peel and dice the carrots. Extract the juice by either puréeing the carrots in a food processor until quite fine, and then sieving through cheesecloth, or passing the carrots through a juice extractor.
2 Measure out 300 ml (10 fl oz) of juice and season with the sugar and salt. Beat the egg white until soft peaks begin to form, then beat into the seasoned carrot juice.
3 Proceed as shown on pages 78–79.

🍴 METHOD

1 Peel and dice the potatoes. Put in a pan of cold salted water and bring to the boil. Simmer until tender, about 15 minutes. Drain well.
2 Return the drained potatoes, still in the hot pan, to the heat for a minute to dry them out. Mash them with a food mill/mouli or a potato ricer. It is important that there are no lumps in the mash. Mash in the butter and season generously.

🍴 METHOD

1 Purée the beetroot in a food processor, then push through cheesecloth.
2 Pour the beetroot juice into a pan and add the sugar and salt. Simmer for 5 minutes. Set aside to cool.
3 Measure out 150 ml (5 fl oz) of the juice into a bowl, and stir in the dried egg white. Whisk until smooth. Cover and refrigerate overnight, or for at least 4 hours.
4 Whisk the juice and egg white mix until stiff peaks form. Proceed as shown on page 132.
For other vegetables, use strained and seasoned juice in the given proportions.

🍴 METHOD

1 Put equal amounts of sugar and water into a pan.
2 Simmer both together until the sugar is just dissolved.

Kitchen schedule planner

The key to successful food presentation lies in the planning. As with many things, preparation is key. Below is a sample menu along with a number of planning and scheduling pointers to give you an idea of the level of preparation required for a three-course meal.

Appetizer

Wild mushrooms and chives in Parmesan basket, with basil foam.

Main course

Shallot marinated fillet of beef in strips, with artichoke puree on a beetroot wafer, and balls of vegetables, basil oil drizzle, and flat-leaf parsley sprigs

Dessert

Chocolate truffle decorated with chocolate flakes, on a sugar plate decoration, served with fresh mango

This particular menu is more suited to winter time, and contains a broad range of flavours that should appeal to most palates. The cooking methods are divided between the hob and the oven, and several of the garnishes can be prepared in advance.

Once you've decided on your menu, go ahead and write your shopping list. You may need to place orders with butchers or grocery shops for some items, so it's important to get this sorted early on. It's also a good idea to purchase any extra decorations you need ahead of time.

THE WEEK BEFORE:

It's best to plan your menu the week before, especially if you will be entertaining a large group or if you are hosting a special occasion. The dishes you decide to have on your menu will be influenced by the season and the availability of certain foods. You don't want to be searching high and low for cranberries the day before your guests arrive for dinner! You may also want to bear in mind the size of your oven – there's only so much you can cram into a small oven. If you think you're going to be limited to the amount of time you can spend in the kitchen on the day, then you may want to prepare some dishes beforehand. When you have a large number of guests to entertain, it's probably easier to make a frozen dessert a few days before, or prepare decorations that you can store, such as sugar sand or sugar wafers for example.

If you're hosting a special birthday or anniversary meal, decorations and garnishes add to the fun and glamour of the party. A frivolous garnish, such as sugar wafers for desserts or savoury foams to dress up your entrées, are great little additions that give your dishes a touch of class. Many of these can be prepared beforehand if you need to save yourself a bit of time on the day.

It's also a good idea to get your dining table plans in order. Think about your table setting, so you know exactly how you plan to decorate your table on the day. You may need to purchase a few little extras to finalize the look you envisage. Check your cutlery and crockery stocks – if they've been stored in a cupboard for months you may want to give them a bit of a clean. Pull out any table linen you need and, if it's been stuck in a musty cupboard, give it a good clean and iron. Most hosts love to decorate their dining table with fresh flowers or herbs. If you plan to have flowers, make sure you order them ahead of time.

THREE DAYS BEFORE:

● Do the shopping for any store-cupboard ingredients, dairy products, or fresh produce that needs to be prepared in advance.
● Make the beet wafers, and store them in an airtight container lined with absorbent paper.
● Make the basil oil and store in the refrigerator.

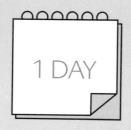

TWO DAYS BEFORE:

● Make the Parmesan basket, and store in an airtight container lined with absorbent paper towels.
● Make the artichoke purée and store in the refrigerator.

ONE DAY BEFORE:

● Collect the beef from your local butchers, and purchase the wild mushrooms, and any other remaining fresh produce and herbs. Wash the herbs in plenty of cold water and store as directed on page 117 for maximum preservation.
● Brush the mushrooms, but do not use water to clean them. Store these in an airtight container lined with paper towels and place in the refrigerator.
● Marinade the beef in a non-metallic container, cover and refrigerate.
● Make the chocolate flakes, and store in an airtight container.
● Make the chocolate truffles.

ON THE DAY:

● Make the basil foam and refrigerate.
● Make the vegetable balls, blanch and refrigerate so they're ready to reheat in boiling water later.
● Select the herb sprigs to garnish.
● Finalize how the mushroom dish and the beef dish will look on the plate – you may choose to make a rough sketch to remind you in the rush of serving up your food to your dinner guests.
● Count the plates and polish them.
● Polish the cutlery. Check the chairs.
● Make a seating plan if appropriate.
● Lay the table.

> **Note:**
> It's useful to keep a record of the event – the date, what was served, who came and how the food was received. This will serve as a useful reminder and resource next time you are planning a menu, especially if you are entertaining the same guests!

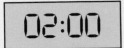

TWO HOURS BEFORE:

- Make the sugar plate decoration, and set aside.
- Chop the chives and mushrooms, and set aside on baking sheets ready to cook.
- Set the Parmesan baskets on a baking sheet ready to warm in the oven.
- Remove the beef from the marinade and set on the baking sheet ready to roast. Keep it refrigerated until then.
- Remove the basil oil from the refrigerator, to allow it to clear before serving.
- Have preparation trays ready for use by your stove.

ONE HOUR BEFORE:

- Preheat the oven for the beef fillet.
- Have the piping bag ready for the artichoke purée.
- Slice the mango finely for dessert.

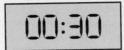

30 MINUTES BEFORE:

- Cook the beef fillet, cover it and set aside to rest in a warm place. Reduce the temperature of the oven for the Parmesan baskets.

15 MINUTES BEFORE SERVICE:

- Cook off the wild mushroom and chive on the hob.
- Warm the Parmesan baskets briefly in the oven. Set out the plates ready for serving. Put the baskets on the plates. Spoon the mushrooms into the baskets, and add any herb garnish. Have the basil foam prepared and drizzle it across the top of the mushrooms just before serving.
- Put the salted water on to boil, so you can reheat vegetable balls.

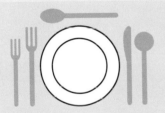

DURING APPETIZER:

- Make sure the entrée course plates are warmed in the oven before serving.
- Have the beef ready to carve on a board, but keep it covered so it stays warm.
- Heat through the artichoke purée on the hob or in a microwave.
- Heat the vegetable balls in the boiling water. Drain and keep warm Have ready the basil oil and the herb sprigs.
- Carve the beef into fine slices.

TO SERVE THE MAIN COURSE:

- Set the beet wafers on the warm plates; add the beef to the plate; pipe on the artichoke purée, spoon the vegetable balls onto the plate; and to finish, drizzle over oil and add the herb sprigs.

TO SERVE DESSERT:

- Simply retrieve the decorated plates, arrange the truffles attractively on the plate, add the flakes, and set the mango on the side. Serve.

Weights and measures

Weights

Metric	Imperial
25 g	1 oz
45 g	1$\frac{1}{2}$ oz
55 g	2 oz
75 g	2$\frac{1}{2}$ oz
85 g	3 oz
100 g	3$\frac{1}{2}$ oz
115 g	4 oz
125 g	4$\frac{1}{2}$ oz
140 g	5 oz
150 g	5$\frac{1}{2}$ oz
170 g	6 oz
175 g	6$\frac{1}{2}$ oz
200 g	7 oz
210 g	7$\frac{1}{2}$ oz
225 g	8 oz
250 g	8$\frac{1}{2}$ oz
255 g	9 oz
275 g	9$\frac{1}{2}$ oz
285 g	10 oz
300 g	10$\frac{1}{2}$ oz
350 g	12 oz
400 g	14 oz
450 g	16 oz (1 lb)
550 g	1$\frac{1}{4}$ lb
675 g	1$\frac{1}{2}$ lb
700 g	1$\frac{2}{3}$ lb
800 g	1$\frac{3}{4}$ lb
900 g	2 lb
1 kg	2$\frac{1}{4}$ lb
1.35 kg	3 lb
1.5 kg	3$\frac{1}{2}$ lb
1.8 kg	4 lb
2 kg	4$\frac{1}{2}$ lb
2.3 kg	5 lb
2.5 kg	5$\frac{1}{2}$ lb
2.7 kg	6 lb
3 kg	6$\frac{1}{2}$ lb
3.5 kg	8 lb
4 kg	9 lb
4.5 kg	10 lb
5 kg	11 lb

Temperature

°C	°F	Gas Mark
3	37	
10	50	
16	60	
21	70	
24	75	
27	80	
29	85	
38	100	
41	105	
43	110	
46	115	
49	120	
54	130	
57	135	
60	140	
66	150	
71	160	
77	170	
82	180	
88	190	
93	200	
96	205	
100	212	
107	225	
110	228	
115	238	
120	250	
130	275	1
150	300	2
160	325	3
180	350	4
190	375	5
200	400	6
220	425	9
230	475	7
250	475	8
260	500	9

Volume

Metric	Imperial	European	American
5 ml	-	1 tsp	1 tsp
10 ml	-	2 tsp	2 tsp
20 ml	-	1 tbsp	1½ tbsp
30 ml	1 fl oz	1½ tbsp	2 tbsp
50 ml	2 fl oz	3 tbsp	¼ cup
60 ml	2½ fl oz	3½ tbsp	¼ cup + 2 tsp
75 ml	3 fl oz	4 tbsp	½ cup (6 tbsp)
100 ml	4 fl oz	¼ pint	½ cup (¼ pint)
150 ml	5 fl oz	¼ pint	¾ cup
175 ml	6 fl oz	-	¾ cup
200 ml	7 fl oz	-	-
250 ml	8 fl oz	⅓ pint	1 cup (½ pint)
300 ml	10 fl oz	½ pint	1¼ cups
350 ml	12 fl oz	-	1½ cups
400 ml	14 fl oz	⅔ pint	1¾ cups
450 ml	15 fl oz	¾ pint	-
500 ml	16 fl oz	-	2 cups (1 pint)
550 ml	18 fl oz	-	2¼ cups
575 ml	20 fl oz	1 pint	2½ cups
600 ml	21 fl oz	-	2¾ cups
700 ml	25 fl oz	1¼ pint	3 cups
750 ml	27 fl oz	-	3½ cups
800 ml	28 fl oz	-	3⅔ cups
850 ml	30 fl oz	1½ pints	3¾ cups
900 ml	32 fl oz	1⅔ pints	4 cups
1 liter	35 fl oz	1⅔ pints	4½ cups
1.1 liter	40 fl oz	2 pints	5 cups
1.3 liter	48 fl oz	2⅔ pints	6 cups
1.5 liter	50 fl oz	2½ pints	6¼ cups
1.66 liter	56 fl oz	2¾ pints	7 cups
1.75 liter	60 fl oz	3 pints	7½ cups
1.8 liter	64 fl oz	3¼ pints	8 cups
2 liter	72 fl oz	3½ pints	9 cups
2.1 liter	76 fl oz	3⅔ pints	9½ cups
2.2 liter	80 fl oz	3¾ pints	10 cups
2.25 liter	84 fl oz	2 quarts	10½ cups

Spoon measures

In American recipes, when quantities are stated as spoons, 'level' spoons are meant. European recipes and those in this book usually call for rounded (neither level, nor over-heaped) spoons, unless specifically stated otherwise. Also, American 'spoons' are standard cooks' measuring spoons, whereas European 'spoons' tend to be available kitchen or eating spoons. The best plan is to regard 2 American teaspoons or tablespoons as 1 English teaspoon or tablespoon. Dessertspoons are not often called for in recipes, but 1 dessertspoon is the equivalent of 2 teaspoons or half a tablespoon.

Index

Credits

Quarto would like to thank the following for kindly supplying images for inclusion in this book:

StockFood: pp. 16t/bl, 17t/bl, 18
Photolibrary: pp. 24, 27, 28, 29
Marks and Spencer (www.marksandspencer.com): p. 25
Alamy: p. 26
Royal Doulton (www.royaldoulton.com): pp. 154–155

We would also like to thank The Conran Shop (www.conranshop.co.uk) for kindly providing us with the plates used in photography.

All other images are the copyright of Quarto Publishing plc. While every effort has been made to credit contributors, Quarto would like to apologize should there have been any omissions or errors – and would be pleased to make the appropriate correction for future editions of the book.